MORE PRAISE FOR SEE, FEEL, THINK, DO

"Great businesses are based on big ideas and, in my experience, the best ideas are driven by instinct rather than analysis. This book gives you the inspiration and confidence to follow your gut."
Charles Dunstone, CEO, The Carphone Warehouse

"Corporations can't do intuition. Entrepreneurs live by it. Andy Milligan and Shaun Smith convincingly illustrate the power and invincibility of original thinking in this admirable book."
Tim Waterstone, founder, Waterstone's bookstores and Daisy & Tom children's department stores

"Those companies that wish to succeed in the Experience Economy should not just See, Feel, Think, Do but also Read. Read what Andy Milligan and Shaun Smith have to say about creating differentiation through unique experience offerings, and then follow through by applying their toolkit to your business."
B. Joseph Pine II and Jam-- -- C-l----- --th--- -f
The Experience Economy

"This book is well overdu┊
instincts, and listening le┊   ┊ore
the customer will benefit.
Jane Shepherdson, CEO, Whistles and former Brand Director, Topshop

"Finally, a book that acknowledges customers are human. By allowing feelings into the forefront of the business process, customer experiences can only improve, which is good news for all of us."
Chris Goossens, Director Customer Service, TNT Express

"A great wake-up call to remind us all that all truly great decisions have been made by people following their instinct."
Richard Reed, co-founder, Innocent Drinks

"Do yourself a favour. Think about buying this book. Feel the beneficial effect of its message. See if you don't."
Professor Stephen Brown, School of Marketing, Entrepreneurship & Strategy, University of Ulster

"My instinct has always been to follow my instinct. It's good to have a book to prove that this works. It's even better that it does so in an engaging way."
John Simmons, brand consultant and author of Dark Angels

"This book voices and exemplifies what many businesspeople think, but find difficult to say publicly. That successful brands and business ideas are born as much from the gut as they are from the numbers. A truly engaging book, with lots of wit and wisdom from people who have felt the force and done something about it."
Rita Clifton, Chairman, Interbrand

"It is very refreshing to read a book on business which is not a how-to, seven-steps-to-heaven management recipe manual, but which instead deals intelligently and with insight on the vague yet vital concept of *instinct* as a business imperative. The notion that proper instinct can be taught seems counter-intuitive, but this book has shown that all our instincts can be better honed and refined so that we can better utilize this for business decisions."
Ho Kwon Ping, founder and Executive Chairman of Banyan Tree Holdings

SEE, FEEL, THINK, DO

THE POWER OF INSTINCT IN BUSINESS
ANDY MILLIGAN AND SHAUN SMITH

Marshall Cavendish
Business

Copyright © 2008 Andy Milligan and Shaun Smith

First published in 2008 by:

Marshall Cavendish Limited
Fifth Floor
32–38 Saffron Hill
London EC1N 8FH
United Kingdom

T: +44 (0)20 7421 8120
F: +44 (0)20 7421 8121
sales@marshallcavendish.co.uk
www.marshallcavendish.co.uk

A CIP record for this book is available from the
British Library

ISBN-10 1-905736-25-8
ISBN-13 978-1-905736-25-6

Designed by So... *www.soitbegins.co.uk*

Printed and bound in Great Britain by
Mackays of Chatham, Chatham, Kent

This book is dedicated to my wife Janine who taught me how to See, Feel, Think, and Do.

Shaun Smith

And this book is also dedicated to my wife Susannah Hart and our boys Ted and Frank – every day they remind me to trust my instinct!

Andy Milligan

CONTENTS

ACKNOWLEDGMENTS

A book such as this has much to do with the hundreds of clients and businesspeople that we come into contact with in the course of our work. Seeing, Feeling, Thinking, and Doing is a process of learning from others as much as it is any original thought on our parts, and there are too many people for us to list them all. However, there are some individuals that we would like to mention specifically for the support, encouragement and help they have given us.

The following people were instrumental in helping us to obtain the case studies and the insights we have used. Stephanie Parry at EMC², Chris Goossens at TNT Global Express, Richard Reed at Innocent Drinks, Abi Carrillo at Vodafone UK, Serra Kanatli at DIA Experience, John Dawson and Carmel McDonald at Dawson McDonald & Associates and Jon Gornstein at Persona Global. Thanks also to Nick Durrant for illuminating us on ethnography and the importance of new research techniques.

Thanks of course to the publishing team of Martin Liu, Pom Somkabcharti, and Linette Tye, and our editor Susan Curran who helped bring the book to market. And finally thanks to Janine Dyer for her patient and persistent project management that ensured we got ourselves organized enough to get this book done!

Andy Milligan and Shaun Smith

SEE, FEEL, THINK, DO
INTRODUCTION

There is a great scene in the movie *The Godfather Part II*. Michael Corleone is visiting Cuba to decide whether he should invest in some mafia-owned casinos there. It is the time of the revolution that would eventually bring Castro to power. His car stops by an alleyway, down which he sees an armed soldier pointing his gun at some guerrillas who appear to have surrendered. Suddenly one of the guerrillas pulls out a grenade which explodes, killing them all. Corleone drives on. Later when he is talking to the mafia bosses, he asks them about the guerrillas. They are dismissive. He tells them what he saw in the alleyway. The bosses laugh, pointing out that it proves how useless and stupid the guerrillas are. Corleone pauses and then disagrees: "It means they can win," he says, and tells them he is not investing.

It is a vignette that shows the power of observation in business (because this was a business deal, after all). Michael Corleone saw something, he felt something which made him think, and that led him to do something that would save him a lot of money. Castro won, and the mafia lost their casinos.

See, Feel, Think, Do: a simple process but a very powerful one.

Business is in fact a simple process: you create something someone wants to buy, they buy it, you take their money and create something else they want to buy, and so on. And underlying the success of business is the simple process of observing and understanding human behavior. The greatest entrepreneurs throughout history have been those who have understood – almost instinctively – what people would value and why, and then delivered it as simply and as easily as possible. The first trader who pitched his stall on a busy road because he understood that people on a long journey must be in need of something to eat or drink was using the power of observation to build a business that met a customer need.

But over the years as markets have evolved and people have become more sophisticated, their needs greater and more emotional, we have begun to see business as not a simple process but a complex one. In fact we have begun to elevate it to a near-science that requires special schooling in arcane techniques such as predicting levels of demand, econometric modeling, strategic planning, value forecasting and that "holy grail" mantra: "return on investment." Business has become so important that we have sought to eliminate the risk from it by believing that if we school ourselves in its best practices and develop rigorous tools for analysis we will be able to follow models for success.

Executives do not even have to bother talking to customers any more: that is "outsourced" to specialist research firms and management or brand consultancies, each with its own tools and processes for extracting the same information from the same customers. All executives have to do now is sit at their desks, attend a few meetings, panic over what the board or shareholders are thinking of them, wait for the research reports or the consultancy recommendation to come in, and press a button marked "Ass covered, now we can go." Except this formula for "job protection" doesn't seem to be working any longer. The average tenure for chief executive officers (CEOs) of large firms in the United States and United Kingdom has fallen to a mere four and a half years. The fact is that there is now a revolving door at the top of most large firms where CEOs come and go, usually with a big payoff despite their poor performance. It's no surprise that employees have become ever more cynical. Short-term thinking, analysts, and research have replaced vision, leadership, and passion in many large businesses today.

But it wasn't always like this. Joseph Cadbury did not sell his chocolate bars on the back of highly engineered research, the first McDonald's was not established on the back of a well-funded management consultancy report and Messrs Hewlett and Packard, Procter and Gamble, and in our own era Gates, Jobs, and Branson did not wait for focus groups and statistical data before launching ideas that would revolutionize the way we work, play and live. They simply saw the world as it was, felt it could be different, thought about how it would be if it were better, and did something about it.

Perhaps that is why four of the five richest Americans dropped out of college: Micorosoft's Bill Gates, the casino boss Sheldon Anderson, Oracle's Larry Ellison and Paul Allen co-founder of Microsoft. Similarly, 19 of the UK's self-made billionaires did not go to university. We shall talk about some of them in this book: Sir Philip Green, Sir Richard Branson and Charles Dunstone all share a common approach to business, one that is much more about DNA than MBA.[1]

The same is true in politics. Love her or hate her (and there were plenty of people in both camps), Margaret Thatcher is still regarded as one of the most successful British prime ministers and admired world leaders in the post-war period. Like it or not, she stood for something. She had a clear agenda based on her observations as a young politician and the problems associated with the overly unionized society in the UK in the 1970s. Thatcher was more See, Feel, Think, Do than political parties today who seem to determine policies more by focus group, photo opportunity, market-tested "sound bites," and MORI opinion polls than old-fashioned belief.

Former chairman of the UK's Conservative Party, Lord Saatchi, launched a withering attack on his party's 2005 election defeat in an interview for BBC Radio 4's *Today* program[2] and criticized his party's reliance on focus groups. (Lord Saatchi is chairman of M&C Saatchi, the worldwide advertising group, and is well aware of the value of consumer research.) He suggested that then Party leader Michael Howard lost the 2005 general election because he lacked a "noble purpose," and went on to say that any future leader should pass a four-point "eye-test" in which a Conservative voter could look them in the eye and assess whether they had a "a noble purpose, there must be a fight against injustice ... there must be a sense of direction ... and there must be a destination." He went on to say, "Look into their eyes and you will immediately discover whether the candidate means it in his answers to those four points or is simply giving you the results of a focus group research report."

This problem is one that not only afflicts UK politicians but, according to Lee Iacocca, is evident in the US too. In his recent book he asks: "Where are the voices of leaders who can inspire us to take action and make us stand taller? What happened to the strong and resolute party of Lincoln? What happened to the courageous, populist party of FDR and Truman? There was a time in this country when the voices of great leaders lifted us up and made us want to do better. Where have all the leaders gone?"[3]

This book is not a criticism of research companies, management consultancies, or MBA courses. It is rather a passionate call to action for all people in business to get back in touch with their instincts and their customers. They must trust their intuition, the knowledge gained and honed through experience over many years, not just in business but in all walks of life. They must make judgments based on information, yes, but also on an empathetic appreciation of any situation. They must see what is there, not strive to find something clever which is not; acknowledge what they feel, not eliminate emotion from the process of judgment; think with a laser-like focus on what is happening and why it is happening, and to do something radical: act referring to research, not because of research. As David Taylor says in his book *The Brandgym*, "Brand bureaucrats use research like a drunk uses a lamp post: for support not illumination."[4]

The power of instinct in business is no better illustrated than by the story of Topshop, one of Europe's leading fashion retailers. This fashion chain, "Once famously naff. Now just as famously cool," as described by the fashion editor of one national newspaper, is one of the best-performing chains on the high street and frequented by celebrity customers like Gwyneth Paltrow, Madonna and Kate Moss. It has become a retailing phenomenon. Much of the brand's success was attributed to Jane Shepherdson, Topshop's former brand director (now CEO of Whistles). She believes that the secret to Topshop's success is the empathy they have with their customers. "We are our customers. We are successful because it is women who are running it."[5] This ability to relate to the customers allows the management team to rely much more on their instinct than research. "Focus groups are okay, but we have got opinions of our own. You have to rely on gut instinct – research is too slow in this business." However, that doesn't mean that they are complacent. Shepherdson and her team visited Sao Paulo to go clubbing and shopping to check out the latest trends and photograph what people were wearing. The Topshop leadership team have little in common with the "paralysis through analysis" school of management. That is why they are so successful.

This book sprang out of our last book together, *Uncommon Practice* (published by FT Prentice Hall in 2002). In that we looked at companies that had created extraordinary customer experiences, and in so doing had created very valuable businesses. We argued that they had been able to do this because they did not follow "best practice." In fact they often rejected it. Instead they did what they felt and thought was right for their brand's customers (not any other brand's customers), and so not only engendered tremendous loyalty amongst their customers and employees, but also in so doing attracted others just like them.

In that book, we noted how these companies relied little on conventional research techniques, and even less on the advice and wisdom of management consultancies. We also noticed what little stock they put on MBAs, other than as an indication of a person's intelligence. (They were much more concerned with DNA than MBA when hiring people.) Instead they tended to rely on their own intuition, informed by but never governed by research. They were able to do this and to be successful because the leaders of the businesses never strayed too far from the source of their profits: the customers. They regularly kept in touch with what their customers were thinking and experiencing by personally experiencing it themselves.

We were asked to help explain this observation in more detail. We wanted to share more stories of how this has been done; to look in more detail at what those companies in *Uncommon Practice* did, and to provide a simple framework that will help others adopt the simple process that we believe is at the heart of success in life and business. Over the last two years we have observed the behavior of many different companies, and researched the stories behind many of the ideas that we are now excited by and familiar with in life. We have also had the opportunity to talk to many leaders and idea creators in business, from restauranteurs to retailers, and from product designers to public transport workers, to glean from them what has inspired them to do what they have done.

From this emerged a simple idea and an even simpler model. In true consultants' style, we labored long and hard over what to call it, and worried about whether we could trademark it. We debated how many stages and steps it should contain, and did our best to over-complicate it. We agonized about its statistical validity and empirical relevance. In short, we allowed ourselves to get far away from the simplicity of the concept, before we hit ourselves on the heads and said, "Hang on. We're falling into the same old trap that most consultants fall into. This is really simple, it's just that it's difficult to do well."

Hence the title of this book: *See, Feel, Think, Do*. As with *Uncommon Practice*, we do not recommend this book for anyone who wants a "just add water" approach to business success. As we have always argued, if there really were only seven steps to success, why aren't there so many more successful people? As we said in *Uncommon Practice*, cook books and management books belong on different shelves. But while the See, Feel, Think, Do concept is simple, it is not simplistic. We have also resisted the temptation of writing a slim book with a big font, with the essential ideas reduced to homilies. There is a place for these, but if you would like to gain insight from the ideas and approaches of inspiring leaders, and if you appreciate a simple, practical framework that helps you to shape your thoughts and translate your ideas into action, then we believe this book will be perfect for you.

So read, feel, think, and do.

WHAT IS SEE, FEEL, THINK, DO?

What we refer to as See, Feel, Think, Do is probably the oldest conceptual model there is in business; in fact it is based on a concept of appreciating human behavior that is probably as old as mankind itself. Put simply, it is the process of observing what someone is experiencing, then using your empathy and intuition, honed by years of experience, to understand what that person is feeling, and finally thinking how the experience can be improved. Simple enough? Good. Now let's make it even simpler – it's about experiencing what your customers experience and changing it for the better.

It requires three key human skills: observation, empathy, and problem solving. And anyone can do it. In fact the more you encourage people in your company to use these natural skills – particularly if they are directly involved in the provision of customer service – the better. Let us give you a small example of how the power of experience works in a real life situation from one of our favorite exponents of Seeing, Feeling, Thinking, and Doing: The Carphone Warehouse, Europe's largest independent cellular phone retailer.

SEE, FEEL, THINK, DO: THE CARPHONE WAREHOUSE'S ULTIMATE PRICE PROMISE

A few years ago Charles Dunstone, CEO of The Carphone Warehouse, noticed a consistent trend in the mobile phone retail marketplace. It was becoming increasingly commoditized and so, just like in any other competitive sector, the retailers were all undercutting the others on price. Dunstone could see just by visiting his stores and those of competitors what was happening and how it was going to affect his customers: a phone that a customer bought in his shop one week could be selling for a much cheaper price as little as a week later. When customer A found that customer B had bought the same phone from the same shop but a week later and cheaper, customer A was likely to be pretty unhappy. Charles used his simple powers of observation and his sense of empathy to begin to think about a solution. He did not conduct any research, he simply thought about what would be the right thing to do to ensure that his customers felt that The Carphone Warehouse was aware of this situation and prepared to stand by its promise of value for money.

The answer was the ultimate price promise. If a customer buys a phone from The Carphone Warehouse and within 90 days the price falls, the customer will be sent a refund for the difference. The finance team at the company blanched at the idea and asked where it would be trialed. Charles said, "If we trial in one store only, it's not fair, so we roll it out across the country." They would launch the scheme in every store. If it didn't work after three months they would pull the scheme from every store. It was simple but risky. In fact Charles told us, "It was the most reckless thing we have ever done." In the first 14 months of operating the ultimate price promise, The Carphone Warehouse gave away £10 million to customers. But what was the result? Customers were astounded when they received unsolicited, redemption vouchers to cover the fall in price. The impact on customer loyalty was enormous, and of course it gave those customers a reason to revisit the store.

Did The Carphone Warehouse measure the specific impact this had had on customer retention or advocacy, then translate this into a return on investment? No, of course not. Charles told us, "It's a great example of something that felt instinctively right." He went on to say:

Most research is generally inconclusive. Most of the things we have done we would not have done if we had researched them. For example, we offered our TalkTalk (landline) customers free calls when calling each other. We could never have proven this would be viable with research beforehand. We had to go with our instinct and trust that customers would recruit others and become more loyal as a result. In fact we now have a million of these customers and have found that the net present value of these customers is twice that of the average and their loyalty level is much higher.

The Carphone Warehouse grew its revenues by nearly 30 percent in 2006. Charles Dunstone is someone who observes what is happening, understands how his customers are feeling, thinks about how to improve the situation for them, and then gets on and does it and in the process increases his profits.

On April 11, 2006 Dunstone announced that TalkTalk customers would enjoy "free broadband." Within 24 hours 20,000 new customers signed up – five times more than anticipated. Despite having tripled call center capacity, The Carphone Warehouse was unprepared leading to widespread customer criticism. By the end of 2006, 2.6 million customers had subscribed to TalkTalk. On this occasion perhaps, "Do" needed more attention. But more of that later.

SEE, FEEL, THINK, DO IN HISTORY

This is of course what we as human beings have been doing since the dawn of time. A mother does it with her child, a husband with his wife, a friend with a friend. We talk about that special "understanding" we have with someone that enables us to read their mood and without asking, say or do something that will make them happier. This level of intimacy does not come through artificial or elaborate research; it comes from the experience of knowing someone and the empathy that engenders. It is this level of intimacy that many companies seek with their customers, and yet they pursue research techniques which actually distance them from the customer.

Throughout history the greatest inventions, the greatest achievements have come from people seeing, feeling, thinking, and doing. We remember the stories that have been told to dramatize this point. Leonardo Da Vinci, for example, saw a bird fly and wondered whether a man could do the same; he built the first flying machines. Remember the story of how Archimedes discovered his principle of displacement? He was getting into his bath and noticed that as he got in, water got out. That simple observation got him quickly thinking, and his shout of *"Eureka"* (which in Greek means "I have found it") signaled his discovery.

The story of Newton discovering gravity is similar. He experienced a simple, everyday event which has happened throughout time: an apple fell on his head. That made him feel something, for sure, but more importantly it got him thinking and subsequently doing something. He established the law of gravity, which has profoundly shaped much of our approach to the physical world ever since.

However apocryphal some of these stories are, they illustrate the point that the most profound discoveries are often made by not only experiencing an everyday phenomenon, but then looking and thinking about it in a different way; a way that is profoundly personal but at the same time capable of being shared with and understood by everyone else. Conversely, we distrust the idea of the scientist locked in his laboratory, experimenting in abstract and artificial surroundings which are removed from "real life." Wizards with their potions, mad doctors with their secret formulas that we can neither understand nor trust, are always portrayed as being removed from the everyday experience of ordinary people. We have, in other words, a quite natural and healthy distrust and suspicion of anything that has not been developed in response to a real need that we can all perceive and understand.

In some ways what has happened in marketing over the years has been the equivalent of handing over the development of products and services to mad scientists locked in laboratories far away from the lives and experiences of the people they are supposed to be creating things for. We have taken a sensible regard for academic intelligence and "cleverness," together with an awe for anything that looks scientific, and elevated it to a primary role in business. Hence the profusion of formulae, Venn diagrams, biaxial matrices, and flow charts that abound in business presentations.

The thinking and approaches of successful business consultancies, such as McKinsey, have been aped and imitated to the point where the perfectly sensible and solid techniques they have developed to analyze problems or frame solutions have been turned into almost immutable laws of business. Asserting the truth of something because you have consistently experienced it is regarded as "flaky" or "unsound." Statistical data which has been put through so called "rigorous models" is now required before any decision can be made. As one Harvard Business School professor told his class, "In God we trust, everyone else brings data."

The problem with this approach is that it has marginalized the role of imagination, of empathy, of trusting "gut instincts" and intuition. It has caused us to lose confidence in making our own decisions based on observing the reality of what is going on around us. It almost requires a child-like innocence untutored by the world of business schools and business processes these days to see things fresh, think things new. It is no coincidence that many of the exciting entrepreneurs of today have had no formal business school training.

None of this is to say that there is not a vital role for measurement, for research, for statistical analysis to help explain and improve things. But it should never have primacy over the time-honored human skills of observation, empathy, and problem solving.

RESEARCH ISN'T WORKING

How did we get here? Put simply, business became so big, so global, and consumers so multitudinous, diverse, and dispersed, that the costs in any business venture (whether it be launching a new product or a new advertising campaign) became so great that companies and the executives who work for those companies needed to use research to mitigate the risk. How can an executive in Procter & Gamble in Cincinnati have an intimate relationship with the millions of customers of the company's products from Seattle to Shanghai?

At the end of the last century, market research was barely embryonic. But because of the very localized nature of business and communications, there was no need for large-scale systematic research. Customers were homogenous, their needs similar, and they tended to be "on your doorstep," so it was possible to ask and understand their opinions and needs, and respond to them quickly.

But with the onset of mass communications and transportation links, it became possible to open up new markets for products very quickly. This meant that manufacturers were now very distant from consumers and unable to know exactly what they were thinking. As the costs of production, distribution, and marketing increased with the reach of new markets, so it became more and more important to get vital intelligence on the suitability or viability of new products or new initiatives with consumers, to ensure that there was a likelihood of success.

The earliest forms of market research were face-to-face or door-to-door questionnaires. These gathered opinions after the fact. When telephones became available, these surveys could be conducted more efficiently and quickly. Opinion polling remained the most widely used form of market research for many years, until its limitations became exposed. It was good at telling you what people thought, but not why they thought that way. The quantity of data gathered needed to be supplemented with richer information exploring why people behaved the way they did. Thus came the rise of the "focus" group and the in-depth interview, where consumers would discuss for up to two hours any issue from what type of washing-up liquid they used to how they voted.

These broad research approaches, quantitative and qualitative, were then populated with a set of tools and techniques in a form of psychological marketing warfare designed to understand the basic motivations and habits of consumers. Raw information was analyzed through an increasingly sophisticated set of statistical and psychological models and indices. The market research industry boomed, and an influx of econometricians, statisticians, psychologists, and psychoanalysts, many with impressive doctoral theses in bewilderingly titled subjects, boosted the intellectual credentials of research. Research became a touchstone for business. Nothing, it seemed, could be done; nothing could be approved, without research. No business was free of an executive demanding, "Have we researched this?" even if that executive had little clue how and what that research should be.

But something disturbing happened. As companies relied more and more on more and more sophisticated forms of research, they began to distance themselves from the very people they needed to know most about, their consumers. As research became more important as an activity in and of itself; it began to override the intuitive decision-making processes that had often made organizations successful. Whether people thought an idea could work or not was unimportant; what mattered was what the research said.

It is still alarming to us now, as we cast our minds back over a combined 40 years of working in business, how many decisions we have seen made by marketers and CEOs based on a set of PowerPoint slides, presented in an airless meeting room, purporting to represent what customers think or will do.

As we have said, this is understandable. The majority of people in business are risk averse. They seek certainties. They have often come from accounting or engineering backgrounds where there are constant sets of results based on given sets of actions. But human beings are messy, unpredictable; marketing to them is fraught with risk. It was inevitable that business people would seek refuge in the certainties of research as a way of eliminating this risk.

The problem was that so much of the research we saw, was flimsy, half-baked, or just inappropriate. Focus groups, which should be used to gain qualitative intelligence, were used as quasi-statistical predictions of behavior. Statistically insignificant quantitative studies were used to provide "insight" into moods and motivations of vast swathes of the population. Given that very few executives in business knew anything about research but knew it was "very important," then as long as any idea had been "researched" (no matter how inappropriate the research techniques), everything was all right.

The result of all this, we believe, is that much research-based decision making has become flawed. Despite all the sophisticated research techniques designed to improve the success rate of new product launches, the rate of failure in new product development has remained constant over the last 20 years at about 80 percent.

A NEW APPROACH EMERGES

But against this trend of over-researched, under-investigated processes, a counter-revolution was occurring, with certain clever researchers at the vanguard of it. They noticed the imperfections in existing research models and techniques. Particularly they were becoming acutely aware of the artificiality of the focus group, the one tool designed above all other to give marketers an in-depth insight into the motivations and aspirations of their customers. They noted the difference between what customers said in focus groups and how they behaved in real life. As Rita Clifton, one-time head of planning at Saatchi and Saatchi and now chairman of Interbrand, put it, "Consumers have a habit of being radical in the research group and reactionary at the check-out counter."

Market research is a rear-view mirror.   **Pantene**

David Taylor, author of *The Brandgym*,[6] says, "Research is a rear-view mirror." He tells the story of the shampoo brand Pantene, which is now one of the leading brands on the market. When it was tested with focus groups prior to launch in 1988, people hated it. "The name sounds like underpants!" they protested. So what did Procter & Gamble (P&G) do? It ignored the research because it had a total belief in the product and thought that with the right advertising, consumers would buy it. So another problem with focus groups is that they reject the new and unfamiliar, and use their current frame of reference to say what they like. Just imagine the response if Richard Branson had said to would-be customers, "I'm starting this new airline with a great business-class product, and thought about calling it Virgin. What do you think?"

LOST IN TRANSLATION

Even when data is collected, it often fails to get to the people who can use it. One company spent close to US$1 million trying to understand what its customers valued. In all, 200 employees in 17 different departments were involved in 105 separate customer research activities. This sounds impressive, but unfortunately there were two major problems. First, the data collection effort was uncoordinated. Some customers were being contacted almost four times a month, and, not surprisingly, they often complained of being asked similar questions by different people for different purposes. The second problem was that the data collected in the company's US$1 million effort was not being used to improve much of anything. It just lay there. Only 43 percent of the people who had collected the data reported it to anyone but themselves. Only 40 percent said any action was taken as a result. Only 27 percent of the information taken from external customers was reported as "acted upon." It was if most of the data so assiduously gathered had disappeared into a black hole.[7]

The final problem is that even when the data is communicated, it may prove of little benefit to the business. It is no wonder, then, that a new survey by Incite Marketing Planning found that half of the segmentation research studies carried out in the United Kingdom have so little value that they are unused by the companies that commission them. Incite concluded, "The implication of this survey is that up to £65 million of spending on such research could be going to waste each year."[8]

So researchers began to look for other methods that might give them a better insight into how people behaved in "real life" situations, and a higher probability that the information could be used to improve the business. And in part their inspiration came from an unlikely source – the world of computer and advanced technology.

"USER RESEARCH" VS "MARKET RESEARCH"

As marketing, the most human of all an organization's processes, was becoming more detached from the people it was designed to serve, so technology was employing more and more techniques to make its products easier to use and more effective to the people they were designed for. In particular, designers of computers began to study at close quarters how people were actually using their prototype products, and then to redesign them to "fit" to the human experience. The inclusion of human factors in the research and development process was called user interface design – a typically "boffin-like" phrase – but it was essentially See, Feel, Think, Do.

In the 1980s as personal computers were becoming more widely available, people seemed reluctant to use them. One probable barrier was simply how "unfriendly" the user-interface screen was – often controlled by a keyboard, the computer would open with a green dot matrix colon and then a quasi-scientific splurge of letters, Ctrl:/F1/Adv or whatever. It was as if the designers of these computers assumed that new users would be reassured by the technological capacity and mainframe heritage that this approach suggested. Then Apple came along and helped popularize the concept of the graphic user interface – the use of a mouse which scrolled a cursor over screen icons to open computers and then open files. It made it simple and friendly and more "human." Apple experimented with different colors, graphics, and sequencing of information before arriving at a user interface that was pleasant, welcoming, and encouraging. The first Apple Macintosh was, it has been said, designed to be roughly the same size and shape as the human head to create a more natural experience. Apple has revolutionized the way we think of personal computers.

This simple approach to design of technology for interface with users had been pioneered years earlier by organizations such as NASA. For example, researchers studied the behavior of pilots in cockpits and noticed that their reaction time to warning signals in the cockpit would be improved if the commands were both displayed visually and also heard. In other words, when there was an "extra channel" that allowed additional information which amplified the impact of the visual signal. Moreover it was the tone and type of language that was used in the spoken commands that was important. A human voice with simple language would be most effective. To this day most voice commands either simulate or are recordings of human voices. This research was not remote, focus group material. It was observation during the actual pilot experience which worked out "what was really going on." This is one simple example of how seeing, thinking, feeling, and doing works.

ETHNOGRAPHY

As well as this empiric approach to observing behavior and designing to fit it, certain researchers were also influenced by a social anthropological technique called ethnography – literally meaning "culture writing." Ethnography is a simple approach but with profound implications. It involves researchers simply watching customers or consumers in the real-life process of purchasing or using products. This might involve standing in supermarkets, watching the way that consumers cruise the aisles, picking up packs, looking at the labeling, putting them back, choosing something else, and so on. Or it might involve accompanying someone on a shop, noting down how he or she behaved. Or it might involve giving consumers a diary to fill in over a week, noting down what they are doing and how many times they use a particular brand, in what circumstances, how they feel about it, and so on. These techniques are called Diary Studies or they can expand into Camera Studies or Cultural Probes.

It is like a "documentary approach" and can involve more "fly on the wall" activities such as the placement (with the approval of the consumers, of course) of cameras in a house to see how people behave. (These are called video or "time-lapse" studies.) More specifically cameras might be located in one area or part of a house, such as the kitchen, to observe the way consumer products are used at home. Some ethnographic researchers have even lived for a week with consumers to get a better understanding of their real-life experiences.

From such observations come new ideas for products or for ways of marketing products. For example, researchers working on a project for a washing powder manufacturer observed that women would typically hold freshly laundered items to their nose and smell them briefly. When asked, the customers said that they judged the cleanliness of the clothes by their "fresh smell." The women were not even aware what they were doing until the observers brought it to their attention, and so could not have articulated this in a focus group, for example. The result was that the manufacturer featured smell as an important part of the washing powder design, and made a point of showing consumers smelling their wash in television advertisements.

One sauce manufacturer, Heinz, saw a problem. Children were the greatest consumers of its ketchup but the people who controlled the use of the ketchup bottle were adults.

Heinz decided on a novel research approach. It involved literally thousands of children in researching how to create a ketchup just for them. Groups of children were brought together in focus groups that were more like "play sessions." Kids love mess, play, funny colors, noise, and shapes. And they love to play with food. In fact they love all of the things that adults "hate" doing and certainly hate their kids doing!

Heinz took their learnings, and designed and developed with the help of the children a range of sauces specifically intended to give kids the permission to play at mealtimes. The bottles were ergonomically designed to be easy to handle by kids (all parents know the feeling when they see a glass bottle tottering in the hand of a five year old). Heinz created a name for the kids' range, inspired by listening to the vocabulary the children used to describe the experience of playing with the bottles. EZ Squirt was chosen to highlight a benefit and to suggest a sense of fun and playfulness. But the real surprise was in the color of the sauce itself, which were chosen by the kids. The most popular color for tomato ketchup among the kids was – green. Subsequently purple and blue were added as range extensions. At the same time, because it came from Heinz and was in easy to use (and keep clean) bottles, the product enabled adults to feel they remained "in control" at teatime.

The EZ Squirt range was a phenomenal success. It recaptured market share for Heinz, and since October 2002 more than 20 million bottles have been sold.

Whether you like the idea of kids pouring purple ketchup over their food or not, the point of this story is that it shows how Heinz employed research techniques that took real consumers in real situations, observed them, understood what was motivating them, and then delivered a solution designed for and in conjunction with them.

SONY AND THE WALKMAN

Sony is another company that, as we shall see later in this book, has encouraged a See, Feel, Think, Do approach in its product development and marketing. The Sony Walkman, now one of the most ubiquitous products in our lives, is an excellent example of this. In the 1970s Akio Morita was a leading executive at Sony in Tokyo. This was a time when the ghetto blaster was making its iniquitous mark on western society. It was born out of the so-called ghettoes of New York and Los Angeles, where young people liked to gather outside, particularly in summer, and listen to music and dance – possibly a reaction to the disco club culture which had become prohibitively expensive for many, and musically exclusive for even more. It began with people opening windows and turning their speakers round so that music blasted out into the street.

Companies, recognizing the need for the music player to be taken into the street, had begun developing portable tape recorders which could give stereo sound performance. These were big and impressive-looking slabs of metal, and soon they were being carried around on the shoulders of young men almost like a weapon or a standard. The ghetto blaster culture was soon aped by the western-influenced young people of Japan. Young people could be seen daily in Tokyo on the streets, in parks, and even sometimes boarding trains with their music blaring out from these unfeasibly large machines.

This was obviously an impractical way of listening to music on the move. Moreover, in Japan it was a culturally insensitive one. The notion of respect in public places and quiet in the company of others is a very important one for many Japanese, and these ghetto blasters contravened those notions. Morita started thinking how he could create music that people could carry round without disturbing the comfort of others. Knowingly or otherwise, he used skills of observation and of empathy.

This is where observation led to insight: if people were carrying the recorders on their shoulders it was because they wanted to listen to the music personally, not because they wanted to share it with others, and certainly not because they wanted to disturb the peace. So Morita used his problem-solving skills. First, these people needed a set of earphones so that they and they alone could listen to the music. Second, they needed the tape player to be so small it could fit into their pocket, so that they could carry it around with them wherever they went. Hey presto! The idea of the Walkman was born. It became a global phenomenon and a part of our daily vocabulary – so much so that in Australia unrestricted usage of the term "walkman" led to the brand name being declared a generic.

When the prototype Walkman was shown to Morita, he allegedly dropped it into a bucket of water, observed the bubbles which rose and said, "There is still too much space – make it smaller." The Walkman came not from focus groups telling marketers what they thought they needed, but from a visionary marketer translating his own everyday experience (seeing, feeling, thinking) into a transformational idea (doing).

Much as the great ideas of our time have come from someone's ability to observe an unarticulated need and act inventively upon it, so some of the great failures have come from someone's inability to read a situation by looking too hard at the wrong thing. The notorious case of Ford's Edsel is an example of this. Throughout the early 1950s the American motor car market had been expanding, with over 7 million cars being sold. Ford had of course been at the forefront of the explosion in car ownership, fueled by its vision of making an affordable car for every American.

In 1954 the company decided to introduce a mid-market car, sitting between its top of the range Mercury and its lower-priced models. This was to be called the Edsel (named after Henry Ford II's father). The aim was to create a new car in a new (mid-market) category. However, instead of looking at the market and thinking about the big picture in terms of the trends and what exactly people would need in future, Ford's researchers decided what typical 1950s car owners wanted. Admittedly they did ask them what they would like in a car, but they never asked how much they would be prepared to pay, and so the car contained lots of features, but at too high a price. Above all, it was decided that what was wanted was a big car with expansive wing tails and new features to make it look different. But the new features were either impractical or unattractive. For example, the automatic transmission buttons (dubbed "Teletouch") were mounted inside the steering wheel, which was where traditionally the horn was mounted. So many drivers were confused and ended up changing gears when they meant to blow the horn. The horse collar radiator grille, later to become infamous, was mounted vertically and was described as looking like a "merc chewing on a lemon."[9]

The car was to take two years to get in production, and by that time, America was on the brink of an economic downturn and drivers were beginning to turn their attention to smaller, more fuel-efficient and well-designed alternatives. In particular Californian drivers were becoming advocates for the iconic Volkswagen "beetle." Ford's researchers dismissed this as being a niche market, and their focus groups convinced them that Middle America wanted more of the same: big, brash, fuel-guzzling automobiles.

The situation for Edsel was not helped by a series of product glitches. Many early Edsels suffered from a number of quality problems: gears were noisy, pumps leaked, brakes failed, push buttons stopped working, hoods stuck, transmissions froze, paint peeled, hubcaps fell off, batteries died, doors refused to stay closed, heaters worked only in summer, and so on (and on). Most of the problems were later corrected, but by then it was far too late.

The Edsel quickly became an expensive joke. Comedians likened its grille variously to a horse collar, an egg, Bugs Bunny, a toilet seat, and even worse, a woman's private parts! A guaranteed joke at the time was, "What can you expect? He bought an Edsel!" The company tried to revive the product with a massive advertising campaign costing almost US$20 million, but the car eventually went out of production in November 1959. After making 110,000 cars, many of which were never sold, Ford had lost around US$250 million.

All right it is easy to be wise after the event. How could Ford have predicted the economic downturn? How could it have known customers' tastes would change? But for us, the key to understanding where it went wrong lies in that phrase: "Ford's researchers had decided" what car drivers wanted. They had looked at the market and said, "This is what people say they want, so let's give them more of that." They were, if you like, following best practice, but they were looking too hard at the wrong data. Did it once occur to them to challenge the norm? Did they once do what Michael Corleone did, actually observe in real life how people were behaving, and ask why? Even when it was clear at the first launch of the car that people were not buying it, the company's strategy was simply to pump in more money to promoting a dying product. Even if Ford was unable to foresee the future when it launched the Edsel, it could have read the signals once it was launched, and either dramatically changed its marketing strategy or simply cut its losses a little earlier than at US$250 million.

The point of this story is that corporate hubris awaits everyone, no matter how great they are, if they don't continue to observe closely what customers are experiencing.

THE LAND ROVER EXPERIENCE

More recently, the concept of "experiential marketing" has thrived. According to a report commissioned by iD, a "live brand agency," experiential marketing can be defined as "a live interaction between a brand and a consumer that is sensitive to the brand's values, impactful, memorable and capable of generating a lasting positive relationship."[10]

Companies as diverse as Lego and Lexus have created consumer experiences that allow customers to interact with the brand in a way that brings alive the brand values. We were visiting a client at Canary Wharf in London recently. Nestled between two huge skyscraper buildings housing the world's largest law firm and largest bank respectively is a public area, and in that area was the "Land Rover Experience." Land Rover had created an off-road experience which allowed customers to be driven around a course that had vehicles climbing impossibly steep inclines, balancing on two wheels and overcoming obstacles that would make the average SAS soldier think twice. The long queue of suited lawyers and bankers waiting for their ride was testament to the success of this event. How many of them subsequently would buy their off-roader to use only as a "Chelsea tractor" for the school run is a different matter. The point is that it certainly brought home the product capabilities and unique values of the Land Rover brand in a way that advertising never could. According to iD, "a staggering 43% of shoppers have purchased a product that they would not have otherwise bought following their participation in an experiential campaign." It is no surprise then that 68 percent of marketers are spending more on experiential marketing in 2005 than they did in 2004, and 89 percent anticipate spending the same amount or more in 2006.

In the following chapters of this book we shall be telling the stories of many different brands from around the world that have kept close to their customers, kept observing and empathizing with their real-life experiences and developing ideas that deliver value. They can be very sophisticated, as with Steve Jobs bringing to market the first commercially successful GUI (graphic user interface) for Apple, or as simple as the example that follows.

We were visiting a riverside bar/restaurant for a drink the other evening. It was a warm Friday evening, and as you might expect, the bar area was overflowing with office workers on their way home, with all tables taken. But as we spoke with the "greeter" we noticed that just off the bar area were many small tables in a large area that was completely empty. We asked to sit there, and were told, "No, because that is our dining area and only available for people wanting to eat." To which we replied, "Well, it is only 6 o'clock. Give it an hour or so and we may well want to eat. But for the moment, since the area is empty, let us at least have a drink." The answer was still "No," so we left, followed by the people waiting behind us.

The result was dissatisfied customers, lost revenue on drinks, and possibly lost diners as well. At some point in the future, the general manager or financial controller might analyze the takings, spot that revenues from the bar peak on warm evenings, and this could cause him or her to question whether the capacity of the bar matches the demand. But then again, perhaps he or she will not. See, Feel, Think, Do would have created a different result. We can see the bar area is full and that the restaurant area is empty. We understand that customers would rather sit than stand, so why don't we open up the restaurant tables to drinkers until dinner guests start arriving? Not difficult, is it?

These examples come from a mixture of our own experience, our own observations, and research we have undertaken specifically for this book. But how can we turn these various case studies and examples into something practical that you as a reader can take away and perhaps use to guide the way you See, Feel, Think, and Do?

SEE, FEEL, THINK, DO: THE MODEL

From the stories that we have experienced or observed, we have arrived at a simple model that we think will help anyone to organize his or her thoughts and approach this subject. Each of the next chapters is given over to an exploration of one of the four areas of the model, and within each chapter we have attempted to deconstruct the process that people have used in this approach. In each stage we have identified three key steps – or let us call them guiding principles, as we do not want to be over-prescriptive. These guiding principles provide a framework and a way of thinking that we believe can *help people in business liberate their approach to business and legitimize good old human instinct.*

We have deliberately chosen simple words and unchallenging phrases to frame our approach. Those of you who have read our earlier books, *Uncommon Practice* and *Managing the Customer Experience*, know that we try not to over-complicate things. Here then is the model and the guiding principles that organize the following chapters:

1. SEE: Walk in your customers' shoes

- **Expert eyes.** Interpret from your own accumulated experiences and intuitions. Make sense of what you see by trusting your own judgment.
- **Soft focus.** Don't treat observing your customers like a forensic, scientific investigation. Instead simply "experience" it. See what is to be seen. Don't get in the way of yourself.
- **Big picture.** Link what you see to the broader context in which it is happening.

2. FEEL: You're a human being too

- **Emote.** Don't be afraid to express or describe what you are feeling about a situation. It's what people do.
- **Engage.** Ask your customers or employees to express their feelings.
- **Empathize.** Close the gap between what you feel and they feel. Understand how similar and different what they feel is from what you feel.

3. THINK: There's no such thing as a stupid idea

- **Cause and effect.** Interrogate like a child why things are the way they are. Be naïve in questioning what factors are affecting the moments when your customers experience your brand. Some of them may be beyond your control; many won't.
- **Perfect world.** Think outside of the box, what is the perfect experience that we can bring customers?
- **"Why?" and "Why not?"** Challenge how this would bring you and your customers real value, and challenge why it can't be done.

4. DO: Make it so

- **Nuts and bolts.** What are the specific things we have to get right and put in place to make the perfect world a reality?
- **Magic dust.** How do we excite our customers about what we are offering them and our people to deliver it?
- **Is it working?** How do we know we have succeeded?

At the end of the book, we add some further structure to this model. In particular we describe the kinds of questions you might need to ask at each stage to ensure you are truly observing, empathizing, and problem solving.

So enough of what See, Feel, Think, Do marketing is. Let's read more about who does it well and how it happens.

SEE:
EXPERIENCE
IT FOR
YOURSELF

It is late; the store shut its doors to customers many hours ago. Footsteps ring out as a solitary figure walks the aisles between silent racks of clothing and waiting displays. That figure is Philip Green, chairman of Arcadia Group, one of the United Kingdom's most successful retailers.

Green learnt his trade many years ago while running under-performing clothing stores and turning them into cash-generating machines before selling them on again. But he is no venture capitalist, merely concerned only with juggling numbers and generating profit regardless of how it is achieved. Philip Green is first and foremost a retailer, and he understands the dynamics of the business intimately.

That is why he sometimes visits his stores late at night. Without distractions, his senses tuned, he can truly experience the store as only a seasoned retailer can. That display is too confusing; that sign is hidden; customers would find it difficult to find that product; why is that litter not cleared? Green recently launched a Kate Moss range through his Topshop brand and spent the night at his flagship London store to experience the buying frenzy for himself. It is this hands-on approach that has led Philip Green to become the fourth richest man in the United Kingdom[11] and the Arcadia group to become the most successful private retailing group in Britain. In the two years after Green bought the group, operating profits tripled to £326 million and he paid himself a £1.2 billion dividend. He is planning to open 100 Topshops overseas in the next three years. However, being hands-on sometimes has a downside. Jane Shepherdson, Topshop's Brand Director left the organization because, it was rumored, she was not consulted before Green hired Kate Moss.

Most chairmen or CEOs rely on hard data like market research and profit and loss accounts to run their business. Green understands that these are vital yet insufficient. They are merely lagging indicators, and therefore fail to give him the insight and early warning that seeing a store first-hand provides. Only direct observation reveals the difference between a store that is well run and one that is not; long before this shows up in the bottom line. That is why Green is famous for being engaged with every aspect of the business, from buying to store locations to merchandising. Experiencing reality yourself is very different from seeing the world through the insulating screen of data. It is the difference between reading the weather report and going for a walk on a beautiful spring day.

As Gordon Ramsay, the Michelin award-winning chef and successful entrepreneur, said in a recent speech, "Customers don't tell you that you are no longer their favorite restaurant. So it is vital to be hands-on and engaged because if you are not you'll find out five or six months down the line when the numbers fall."[12]

Ramsay's approach, like Philip Green's, is about seeing for yourself. *It is the antidote to two-inch-thick research reports, two-by-two grids and too-smart young MBAs.* Ramsay applies this pragmatic approach to helping ailing restaurants in the television show *Ramsay's Kitchen Nightmares*. Each week Gordon Ramsay is tasked with helping a restaurant that is failing for one reason or another to turn around. He uses a simple yet absolutely consistent approach. First he spends time in the restaurant seeing for himself; observing the experience, and using his own expertise to diagnose the problem. Then he spends time talking with customers and employees, asking them how they feel about the restaurant and the people who work there. Often by this stage he has a gut feeling about what the underlying issue is, and will test his early diagnosis with the manager and staff. It is also at this point that we see Ramsay doing what he does best; making his feelings absolutely clear about what he is experiencing and why it must change.

His next step is to think about what it would look like if it were better from the customer perspective. Frequently, this is about simplifying the menu, changing the service style and rethinking the pricing. Only then does he start doing anything. Often he will give the chef a night off and demonstrate new dishes himself. He makes it absolutely clear what is required and the consequences of failure. He scolds, praises, coaches, then finally hands back the reins to the management team while he takes a seat in the restaurant to experience the new service with invited guests. His final step is to visit the restaurant several months later to check on progress. Usually, although not always, Ramsay is able to improve the fortunes of the restaurants featured. He doesn't use focus groups, consultants, or pore over the financials. He Sees, Feels, Thinks and then Does.

The Cheyenne, Native Americans, have a saying:

Do not judge your neighbor until you walk two moons in his moccasins.

The modern equivalent of this is the process of experiencing reality from your customers' perspective. You must see your product as they see it; be treated as they are treated; feel about your brand the way they feel. All too often senior executives are insulated from the reality that their customers experience.

Some years ago we were consulting to a large international hotel brand that had been falling behind its competitors in terms of the customer experience. We were asked to facilitate a two-day strategy session for the president and his direct reports at one of the group's properties on Miami Beach. We arrived at the hotel, and no sooner had we given our names than we were taken straight to a suite on one of the top floors and registered there. Over the course of the next two days the group enjoyed a series of wonderful lunches and dinners, served in a private room, culminating in an elaborate farewell dinner cruise on board a yacht that once belonged to President Kennedy. During his after-dinner speech the hotel president said, "You know, some of the reports say that our service is lacking, but I reckon it is pretty darn good." He really did not know that the service we had experienced was far removed from the reality of his customers. The fact was the hotel general manager had been working for weeks to ensure that everything was just right for this event, and we were considered VIP guests for all of the employees.

Jack Welch, the former CEO, defined the dysfunctional organization as one where the "employees have their face towards management and their ass towards the customer." One way to prevent this internally focused culture is to ensure that the leaders of the organizations are as close to the customers as their employees are and do not turn their first-hand observation of the operation as a "Presidential visit."

DAVID NEELEMAN:
WALKING IN MOCCASINS AT JETBLUE

It is an evening flight from New York to Oakland, California. The flight attendants are passing through the aircraft passing out snacks, but one, an older man with graying hair, pauses to speak with many of the passengers that he serves. His name is David Neeleman, and he is founder and CEO of US airline JetBlue Airways. Unlike most airline executives who prefer the privilege and anonymity of flying in seat 1A, Neeleman prefers to work his passage, spending time with his customers to experience what they experience, talk to them about their businesses, and listen for the big ideas. Having put in a day's work in his office, spending five and a half hours serving and talking with customers is not an easy option. But then Neeleman is not the kind of executive who believes that there is a substitute for talking with customers first hand. "I get most of my ideas on flight like this one," he said in an article for *Inc.* magazine.

Neeleman's ideas run to offering the lowest fares in the industry, live satellite television on board flights, and leather seats because he once spent an entire flight sitting on a urine-soaked seat and vowed never to fit fabric seats in his aircraft. These initiatives have resulted in JetBlue being voted Best Domestic Airline by *Condé Nast Traveller* magazine three years in succession, and have propelled the company to US$1 billion in revenues from its start-up in 1999. This is still tiny compared with the likes of United, American Airlines, or Delta, but how many of these carriers have had 12 consecutive profitable quarters over the period post-September 11, 2001, when the US airline industry fell in a tail-spin? While US Airways and United fell into bankruptcy, JetBlue achieves among the industry's best operating margins, seat utilization factors, and one of the top rates for on-time arrivals. In its 2004 Airline Quality Ranking Survey, the University of Nebraska rated JetBlue "Best US airline."

Neeleman is first and foremost an entrepreneur, so much so that he and Dave Barger, JetBlue's president and COO, jointly received the US National Entrepreneur Program Entrepreneur of the Year award in 2003. However, the two men are as chalk and cheese. David Neeleman is not a big-company man. In fact after he left his executive vice-president job at Southwest Airlines he went on to create Open Skies, a company that develops airline reservation systems, which was later sold to Hewlett-Packard. Neeleman then went on to start WestJet, a low-cost carrier in Canada. His forte is seeing the market opportunity and then creating the proposition to meet it. He does this through his hands-on style and ability to engage directly with customers and employees. But the airline industry is not one that allows a lack of attention to detail, and Neeleman recognizes that he needs a partner who knows how to manage complex businesses using hard data.

This is where Dave Barger comes in. While Neeleman looks at the big picture, his partner Barger spends hours poring over the operational data, ironing out problems, reviewing what time the last bag was delivered to the arrivals area, flagging certain flights as "focus flights" which require an in-depth analysis of why they were delayed. It is this combination of soft focus and hard data that has made the team such a winning combination. Neeleman understands this. "I'm not the guy to oversee the day to day," he told *Fast Company* magazine.[13] "That's Dave Barger. He loves that. I'm looking for the new deal, the new technology. My passion is making sure our product stays fresh and exciting, and that we keep our costs low."

Neeleman and Barger have big ideas for JetBlue. Within seven years they plan to have 290 planes and 25,000 employees, and they are currently adding a new plane every three weeks. Growth of this kind presents a whole range of different difficulties, as Peoples Express Airlines found back in the 1980s. This organization revolutionized air travel with its blend of low fares and customer focus. The problem was it could not make the transition from small start-up to large mature business. Time and unforeseen operational pressures will test if JetBlue is able to do so but there are large companies that have experienced growth pains, survived, and thrived: companies like Harley-Davidson, for example.

HARLEY-DAVIDSON: SUPER-ENGAGEMENT

2004 saw the 100th anniversary of Harley-Davidson. The brand has much to celebrate. It has delivered nearly 20 consecutive years of record earnings and revenues. In 2002 shareholders realized a five-year total return of 242 percent. As we write this edition, Harley-Davidson continues to announce record earnings of $5.8 billion achieving a 16.3 percent increase in sales in the Japanese market.

It is hard to believe that this company had a near-death experience in the early 1980s and was close to giving its market to the Japanese manufacturers. The turnaround can be traced back to 1981, when a group of 13 senior Harley executives, led by Vaughn Beals, bought the company. They celebrated with a victory ride from the company's factory in York, Pennsylvania, to its headquarters in Milwaukee, but this was just the first step of a journey that was to see the company transform the way it does business. The journey saw the management team adopt the principles of See, Feel, Think, Do, though they may not have thought about it in quite those terms.

The Harley-Davidson recovery began with engaging with the hard-core enthusiasts who had stayed with the company through the bad times of poor product quality and indifferent after-sales service. The first thing that Richard Teerlink did when he took over as the new CEO was to tap into this rich asset – the people who cared about the Harley-Davidson brand. He asked the question, "How can we create more value for our customers so that they will willingly buy more of our products and services?" To answer the question he started spending time with the loyal customer base and inside the company with its workforce. The result was the Harley Owners Group, started in 1983, which today numbers 850,000 members worldwide.

Rich Teerlink and his management team set out to develop a profound understanding of the experience the company was providing by riding with their customers on a regular basis. All Harley executives were set the target of riding with customers at least 10–15 days each year. They called this program "super-engagement." They wanted to find out first-hand what customers expected. What did they experience? What would make the experience better? How could the Harley promise of "We fulfill dreams" be brought alive?

What Teerlink and his team discovered was that customers loved the look and feel of the bikes, the image of the brand, and the sense that the products were different from any of the competitive offers. What customers hated were the unreliability, poor quality control, and uncaring after-sales service. Most importantly, the management team found out that there was a passion for the brand and a desire to make it great again.

This process of seeing first-hand what customers were experiencing and empathizing with how they were feeling led the management team to evaluate their strategy for the brand and develop an action plan for recovery. They realized that they had to improve product quality as a first priority, then design new bikes that continued the distinctive Harley look and feel (including the famous engine sound), but boasted the performance of the latest Japanese sports bikes, with handling to match. The sales and after-sales experience were improved, and new merchandise and services were introduced: clothing, vacations, rentals, and the Rider's-Edge program, a bike-handling course designed to attract new riders.

Having had a near-death experience once, Harley-Davidson is not about to risk losing touch with its customers a second time. The organization now keeps abreast of changing customer needs through its "Super-engagement" process. Managers continue to ride with customers on a regular basis to hear their feedback directly. An important business metric is participation in Harley Owners Group events. So if 20,000 people participate in a weekend ride in Austria this year, the organization sets the target to increase attendance next year. This passion for seeing how customers use the products first-hand and understanding how they feel about the experience through participating in the same events has led to Harley-Davidson creating a brand community where customers, managers, and employees come together to celebrate their passion for biking. John Russell, managing director and VP of Harley Davidson Europe, sums it up this way: "Every company probably has their real brand enthusiasts, their loyalists, but I think what Harley has been able to achieve is that we've made them a very significant proportion of the ownership."[14]

ST LUKE'S: WALKING IN CLARKS SHOES

Walking in moccasins is a technique used by leading advertising agencies to get their creative staff to really understand their client's brands. For example, Phil Dourado and Phil Blackburn in their book, *Seven Secrets of Inspired Leaders,*[15] tell the story of how St Luke's, the leading London-based advertising agency, has created the "Clarks Room" for its client Clarks the shoemakers. The room is themed around shoes; even the coffee table wears shoes; the legs on the table are thoughtfully fitted with small pairs of Clarks! This is where account meetings take place and creative brainstorming sessions are held, surrounded by visual clues that reinforce the client's view of the world. This is a wonderful way of reminding people of what their client's business is all about but it is not a substitute for truly experiencing what customers experience.

Ironically, Harley-Davidson used a Japanese technique to improve its business and win market share from Japanese manufacturers. This technique is described by the Japanese term *gemba,* which means "going to where real actions take place." So the chief executive's office is not gemba, but a store is. Masaaki Imai, the founder of the Kaizen Institute and author of *Gemba Kaizen: A commonsense, low-cost approach to management,*[16] talks about the importance of going to the actual place, seeing the actual situation, making actual improvements, and not asking for ideas. This last point may be surprising, but if you think about it one of the limitations of market research is that customers "don't know what they don't know." They may be able to articulate what it is that they do not like, but rarely are they able to tell you how it should be improved, beyond generalities like "better displays" or "friendly people."

One small example of this is supermarket shopping bags. There is a very good chance that you have found yourself at a supermarket check-out desperately trying to pack shopping bags as quickly as the sales assistant is scanning your purchases. You fill one bag and grab another, only to spend what seems like minutes, but what probably is only 10 or 15 seconds, trying to find the opening. The sides of the flimsy plastic seem welded together and defy you to prise them apart. This small scenario gets played out in supermarkets all over the world every day, and it is highly unlikely that it ever gets mentioned in customer satisfaction surveys; first because the supermarkets don't think to ask about it, and second, because customers think that it is such a trivial detail, albeit a very irritating one at the time, that they do not complain about it. The managers at Tesco, the UK's largest supermarket and the biggest online grocer in the world, decided to do something about it, because 10 seconds a bag multiplied by the 12 million customers that use them every week adds up to a lot of lost time and irritation. Tesco has now introduced a new type of bag with a red tab at the top. The customer pulls this tab and the bag comes off the rack already opened; it is simple but ingenious. It is no accident that Tesco's brand promise is "Every little helps."

So walking in our customers' moccasins helps us see the world through their eyes so that that preconceptions and assumptions do not affect the picture. At the same time it requires being able to see with an expert eye. Philip Green can look at a display and see it as a customer, but also know what needs to happen to make it better. David Neeleman can work a flight and find a new business opportunity. So what are the guiding principles you should bear in mind when walking in your customers' moccasins? We think there are three:

- **Expert eyes**: interpret from your own accumulated experience and intuitions; make sense of what you see by trusting your own judgment.
- **Soft focus**: don't treat observing your customers like a forensic, scientific investigation. Instead simply "experience" it. See what is to be seen, don't get in the way of yourself.
- **Big picture**: link what you see to the broader context in which it is happening.

EXPERT EYES

Interpret from your own accumulated experiences and judgment; make sense of what you see by trusting your intuition.

Take any professional who has spent years perfecting his or her craft, and he or she will have a sixth sense about a situation. Professionals can look at something that you or I might observe but see it in quite a different way. Through their years of training and observation they develop expert eyes which enable them to quickly assess a situation and understand what is wrong. Police officers have this ability. So do fire officers. So do airline pilots. In these cases their exposure to potential danger develops a sixth sense that equips them with the ability to know when something is wrong and what needs to happen to make it right. But this same ability can be developed in any field of activity, provided that the accumulated experience does not cause people to see what they expect to see, rather than what is really there.

Gordon Ramsay uses the expert eyes of his team to maintain his competitive advantage "When a major new restaurant opens anywhere in the world I book a table for six within 48 hours of its opening. Three of my waiters and three of my chefs dine there so that we can stay ahead of the latest developments."[17]

The ability to trust your expert judgment rather than rely on analysis is well illustrated by Malcolm Gladwell in his book *Blink*.[18] Gladwell relates the story of a marble sculpture called a *kouros* dating from the sixth century BC which was offered to the J. Paul Getty Museum in California for a cool US$10 million. *Kouroi,* as they are known in the plural, are extremely rare items, and US$10 million is not an insubstantial amount, so the Getty museum was very cautious. It took the sculpture on loan, and for the next 14 months subjected it to extensive scientific testing. A geologist from the University of California examined the statue with a high-resolution stereomicroscope. He took a small sample from it and analyzed it using an electron microscope, electron micro-probe, mass spectrometry, X-ray diffraction, and X-ray fluorescence. Its provenance was scrutinized and checked against all known records, and finally the Getty Museum was satisfied. Every piece of data and all the analyses pointed to the sculpture being authentic. In late 1986 the statue went on display for the first time, and the occasion was marked by with a front-page story in the *New York Times.*

Some while later Thomas Hoving, the former director of the Metropolitan Museum of Art in New York, was invited to view the sculpture. According to Gladwell the first word that popped into Hoving's head when he saw the sculpture was "fresh." This is not the obvious description for a two thousand year old statue. Yet so strong was his reaction to seeing it for the first time that his advice to the J. Paul Getty curator was, "Try to get your money back."

As it turned out further analysis showed that indeed the statue *was* probably a fake that had been artificially aged. The point is that the 14 months of testing and analysis of hard data had failed to achieve what a few seconds' observation using expert eyes had revealed.

Why then do so many experts get fooled by data? The answer is that we tend to over-estimate the importance of data and under-estimate the importance of intuition. We often see what we expect rather than what is really there, and sometimes the more experienced we are, the greater danger there is of this happening. When Thomas Hoving saw the statue he reported that the word "fresh" popped into his mind. He was using expert eyes to see the statue, but there was something else happening too: he was experiencing the reality of this statue on this occasion, not simply seeing what he expected to see, colored by the extensive research that had been conducted.

The problem with much of our business school system is that it downplays the importance of hard-won experience in favor of empirical data. In an article published in the *Harvard Business Review*,[19] Warren Bennis and James O'Toole argue that there is a crisis brewing in management education because business schools have adopted a scientific model that assumes business is an academic discipline like chemistry or geology, rather than a profession like medicine or the law. As a result most of the business schools hire professors based on their academic prowess and the number of articles they have published, rather than their experience in industry. In fact, Bennis and O'Toole say, "Today it is possible to find tenured professors of management who have never set foot inside a real business, except as customers." They go on to conclude that "the problem is not that business schools have embraced scientific rigor but that they have forsaken other forms of knowledge."

SOFT FOCUS

Don't treat observing your customers like a forensic, scientific investigation. Instead simply "experience" it. See what is to be seen, don't get in the way of yourself.

Have you ever seen one of those maddening pictures made up of swirls of color that are supposed to reveal a picture when viewed in a particular way? They are called stereograms, and are in fact three-dimensional images formed from a series of colorful shapes. The more you try to see the image, the more elusive it becomes. We were never able to "see" the image in these pictures until someone taught us the trick of using "soft focus." As you look at the picture you allow your focus to go soft. In other words, rather than focusing on the picture or the components of it, you "look through" it and try not to see anything. And then something miraculous occurs. The pattern seems to rearrange itself, and suddenly a three-dimensional image swims into focus.

Chemist Friedrich Kekule, who discovered the molecular structure of benzene, did something like this one day while sitting by the fire. As he gazed into the fire contemplating a problem, he looked at the flames with "soft focus." As he did so the twisting and turning flames dissolved into atoms which reformed into a snake. The snake appeared to grasp its own tail and whirl before his eyes. It was at that moment that Kekule intuited the structure of the benzene ring.[20]

The sculptor Rodin was allegedly asked how he was able to create such life-like statues. His reply was, "I just chip away those bits that don't look like a figure." So soft focusing is the ability to see beyond that which is in front of your eyes and perceive at a deeper level. It engages your subconscious to work in concert with your vision.

Sometimes, trying too hard to analyze data stops us seeing what there is to see. When we truly experience something our senses feed us data without the straitjacket of our expectations getting in the way. The business equivalent is seeing a new opportunity through observing customers in soft-focus mode, but then having the discipline to turn this into a business opportunity.

Tim Waterstone, the founder of Waterstone's bookstores and Daisy & Tom children's department stores, told us, "Marketing starts with yourself; you then hope that there are a million out there like you." The best use of research is to quantify what your gut tells you is an opportunity. You should not expect it to create the opportunity for you.

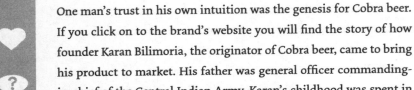

COBRA BEER: RESEARCH STARTS WITH YOU

One man's trust in his own intuition was the genesis for Cobra beer. If you click on to the brand's website you will find the story of how founder Karan Bilimoria, the originator of Cobra beer, came to bring his product to market. His father was general officer commanding-in-chief of the Central Indian Army. Karan's childhood was spent in and around the officers' mess, and this was also the place that he first experienced beer. The website tells the story this way:

> It was a place to observe people and beer. He would hear frank opinion on food, wine and beer. It was market research before there was such a thing. It was here that he began to think about a beer that would not be just another beer.

It was years later that the young Bilimoria, while studying law at Cambridge, experienced that staple of the student throughout the United Kingdom, curry and lager. However, the beer on offer did not match up to his standards. "The trouble with all the beers that I tasted was that they left you gassy and bloated, with not enough room for your food." Inevitably he recalled his early market research in his father's mess, and at the age of 27 started importing beer from India. His first container landed in the United Kingdom at the height of the recession, and in a beer market that is one of the most competitive in the world. He also found that he had to overcome the problem of his beer being shipped in large bottles when the market was used to small bottles. He turned this to advantage by pointing out the benefits of buying larger bottles and sharing them with a friend. After numerous struggles business grew, and finally, after five years revenues hit £1 million a year. However, profitability was another story, with over 50 percent of management time being absorbed with shipping beer over from India.

The answer was to brew in the United Kingdom. Bilimoria placed his business with a family-owned brewer in Bedford called Charles Wells, and today the beer is available in supermarkets, off-licenses, and bars. Despite the overall beer market declining with the growth in wine consumption, the premium end of the market is strong, and Cobra has plenty of room for expansion. The Cobra beer story illustrates the power of observation coupled with the vision to see new business possibilities, and finally the tenacity to execute.

Tim Waterstone's mantra that "marketing starts with yourself" was certainly something that Scott Livengood, CEO of Krispy Kreme, embodied. He was also lucky that there were more than a "million out there just like (him)."

KRISPY KREME: A LITTLE BIT OF MAGIC

Some people look at donuts and see a sweet bun with a hole in the middle. Some people look at a donut store and see a place where donuts are sold and sometimes made. But Scott looked at the store and saw a theater where he could create a little bit of magic.

Livengood was leading Krispy Kreme when its ailing retail performance was seriously affecting prospects for survival. He and his team turned the performance of the brand round by the power of simply observing their business through the eyes of their customers. Krispy Kreme donuts are unique. They are made using a yeast and cake mix which gives them a succulent sponge-like quality. But though people loved the donuts, they were not visiting the stores as often as in the past. And when you have a brand where the freshness of the product is critical, you need people buying when the product has just arrived in your stores.

Scott and his team did of course have lots of sales data showing what was happening with performance, and they had masses of quantitative information about what customers did and didn't like. But what they lacked was the answer to the question, "Why won't more people come into our stores?" That answer came from observing for themselves what customers actually experienced in the stores, and asking them what was special about that experience. By visiting the stores, the team saw that the moment customers got excited was when they saw their donut come out from the kitchen, piping hot, through a little hole in the wall behind the counter. Why was this? He put himself in the customers' shoes. After all, he loved the donuts too. That was the key point: he "loved" the donuts. The donuts smelled wonderful, tasted great because they were baked in a special way. And didn't "a million people just like him" want to see how they were baked, see their donut, their fresh donut, get made? It's why small children like to hang around the kitchen when chocolate cakes are being baked: they are eager for the end product of course, but it's the smell; the magic of seeing the mix rise and brown; the "ping" of the oven alarm when the cake is ready; and the delicious aroma when the cake emerges hot from the oven. It is the whole magical experience that teases their taste buds and leaves a warm glow, not just the cake itself.

Scott and his team realized that the experience in the store was a magic moment. Seeing the process of fresh donuts being made not only delights the senses and raises expectations, it also means that customers can see with their own eyes that they are getting a fresh quality product – it is being made right in front of them.

Scott Livengood had walked in his customers' moccasins, and he had also used "soft focus." He had stopped analyzing and instead just opened himself up to the reality that was in front of him all the time. Scott and his team took that learning and did something very powerful with it. They completely re-engineered the whole store experience, making the donuts became the centerpiece of the store, a process which every customer could see and which would be celebrated with theatrical touches. They changed the time when the donuts were made to the times when most customers were passing by the store, at breakfast time and in the late afternoon. The smell of the fresh donuts was pumped out into the street, inviting people to follow its alluring scent. A big red neon sign flashed "Fresh donuts" when a new batch was ready, and the whole of the kitchen area was opened up so that everyone could see the donuts being made fresh for them. Finally a conveyor belt carrying the donuts was led right past the customer area so customers could see "their" donut being delivered.

How do you continue to walk in your customers' moccasins when you have 200 stores (of which 125 were franchised at that time) and a very complex multi-sensory process? Rather than rely on surveys, Scott gave digital cameras to all of his store inspectors, and sent them out to assess the experience through the customers' eyes, and send back the photographs so that he and the management team could "see" the experience virtually as well as from their own store visits.

Krispy Kreme staff were encouraged to share their customers' passion for donuts, and communicate the sheer theatrical fun of the experience. They even appointed an official "Master story teller" to capture and share customer stories. The result was a nationwide phenomenon in the United States. When a new Krispy Kreme store opened, people could be found queuing around the block overnight just to be first in the store and see those donuts which, in the words of a song written about the brand by one customer, are so great that "even the hole tastes good."

SEE THE BIG PICTURE

Link what you see to the broader context.

Dr David McClelland of Harvard University conducted a survey of star performers at the highest executive levels, and compared them with average performers. He found that technical expertise and intellectual ability were not distinguishing factors in separating the two groups, but "big picture" thinking was. This ability was 13 percent greater among the stars.[21]

This finding is certainly illustrated in the investment market. Rudolph-Riad Younes, head of Julias Baer's international fund, has achieved one of the world's most impressive investment records. He has produced an average return of nearly 15 percent a year for the past 10 years. In an interview with the *Sunday Times* (July 10, 2005) he said, "Most portfolio managers think they are just analysts who just pull a trigger to buy or sell stocks.... But if they do their job properly, they should be a combination of strategist, analyst and trader." The strategist part is about seeing the big picture: looking at the whole forest, as he put it.

Younes also talks about the division between the left (rational) and right (creative) hemispheres of the brain. He believes both are needed:

We are not so smart that we can beat the market using only half our brains. The big picture is important but it's not everything, and it's the same with the close-up picture [what we would call expert eyes]. You have to balance, to be selective and open-minded.

The problem for many professional managers is that they have been trained to rely on their rational skills rather than their creative ability. Somehow we believe that rational is good, and creative is flaky – OK for advertising people perhaps, but proper businesspeople just need to be good at the numbers. This thinking is particularly prevalent in the US and UK cultures. Mark Ritson, associate professor of marketing at Melbourne Business School, said recently, "As Anglo-Saxons, we take great pride in our rationality, having a love of numbers and research-driven thought. In our view, good managers reject their instincts and rely on market research and strategic analysis." He went on to say, "Our Latin counterparts take a much more cynical view of market analysis, viewing it as a backward step, with the result that they excel in industries for which creativity is key."[22] Perhaps this is why nine of the 10 most valuable luxury brands are Latin-owned.

The Krispy Kreme story shows the power of using soft focus to see new possibilities and expert eyes to operationalize them. But it also illustrates the importance of keeping the big picture in mind in order to deal with changing circumstances. Krispy Kreme's insight was in understanding that customers wanted to experience fresh donuts made in-store. The introduction of in-store production led to it selling as many donuts as its rival Dunkin' Donuts with about a twentieth as many outlets, and earning approximately five times the sales income per store in 2003. Krispy Kreme's listing on the New York stock exchange was the most successful initial public offer ever at that time.

Unfortunately, soon after it saw a decline in its fortunes and a collapse in its share price, partly because it failed to react quickly enough to the move towards low-carb foodstuffs, and also suffered from poor management of the resulting slide in revenues. While the Krispy Kreme experience is highly differentiated and a lot more compelling than its competitors, the fact is that the market as a whole has moved away from high-fat products. The bigger picture is one of a softer market, and Krispy Kreme was criticized for failing to manage properly in this more difficult trading environment. Stephen F. Cooper was named CEO, replacing Scott Livengood. Time will tell if Stephen Cooper and the new team manage to See, Feel, Think, and Do their way back to Krispy Kreme's once-exceptional place in the US market.

Don Henshall managing director of Krispy Kreme UK said, "If I have learnt anything from this, then it is that I don't want to overstretch myself. In three years Krispy Kreme went from having sales of about $100 million to $600 million and they floated. *The management took their eye off what really mattered.*"[23]

VIRGIN: BLUE SKY THINKING

Failing to see the big picture is not something that Sir Richard Branson has ever suffered from. The Virgin Group has grown through spotting those markets where traditional thinking, poor service, and "fat-cat" companies have dominated. Branson has made a business from entering these industries and, in his own words, "daring to be daft": in other words, differentiating through offering better service, better prices, and more customer-friendly practices. He told us that he started Virgin Atlantic because "I was jumping on and off planes and I couldn't find one positive redeeming factor about any of the airlines I flew on. I felt we could set up an airline that treated people as human beings and was a pleasure to fly …."

When Virgin Atlantic entered the airline market the industry was dominated by the large national carriers, which were technically competent but were not noted for seeing the world through their customers' eyes. For example, most airlines believed that the travel experience begins at check-in. Virgin Atlantic mapped its customer touchline and realized that in fact the experience begins with leaving home or the office for the airport, and that the journey is often stressful and not a good start to the experience. As a result Virgin introduced complimentary limousine pick-up service for its business passengers, and will even collect baggage from hotels to avoid passengers having to worry about this.

This wider view of the customer journey helped Virgin to see the big picture, take a fresh look at the whole experience, and try to make it more entertaining, less stressful, and more distinctive. Think of any airline lounge and what do you see? Muted colors, rows of soft chairs, a large-screen television tuned to CNN, a few newspapers and business magazines. Think again. How about a ski simulator to help you brush up on your parallel turns? How about practising your golf swing whilst you wait for your flight? How about a branded hair salon? When Virgin researched these ideas they were told by customers that they were of no value. The airline bet that the research was negative simply because these initiatives were so far removed from what customers had experienced. So Virgin introduced the ideas anyway, because they were an integral part of the Virgin experience and a way for the brand to differentiate. The customers loved them. Once again, Virgin had looked at the status quo and seen it through fresh eyes. It is no surprise then that Branson's latest venture is to take the brand literally out of this world. He has teamed up with an aviation designer and inventor of Spaceship One, Burt Rutan, to launch Virgin Galactic. If all goes to plan, anyone with £100,000 to spare can fly Virgin Galactic into space.[22]

Recently Virgin has been trialing the Gibbs Aquada, an amphibious car that converts into a speedboat. Those of you who have ever traveled from the City of London to Heathrow will know that congestion is a major hassle, so Virgin are looking at using these vehicles to transport their customers from their offices in the City to

Heathrow along the River Thames. Result: the journey is less hassle, more fun, different – all the things the Virgin brand stands for, in fact. And this is an important point: innovation that is disconnected from the strategy for the brand is merely a gimmick, and one that is unlikely to survive the test of time. Many other airline chiefs would have seen the Aquada and perceived no benefit. Branson saw it, and immediately connected it with the brand experience that he wishes to create for his customers. We shall see if it stands the test from being an insight to being a product that can be executed on a regular basis, but that is the subject of a later chapter.

So See, Feel, Think, Do. Each of the stories in this chapter illustrates all of these elements to a greater or lesser extent. Each element is dependent on all of the others for complete success, but without the ability to see, none of the others become possible.

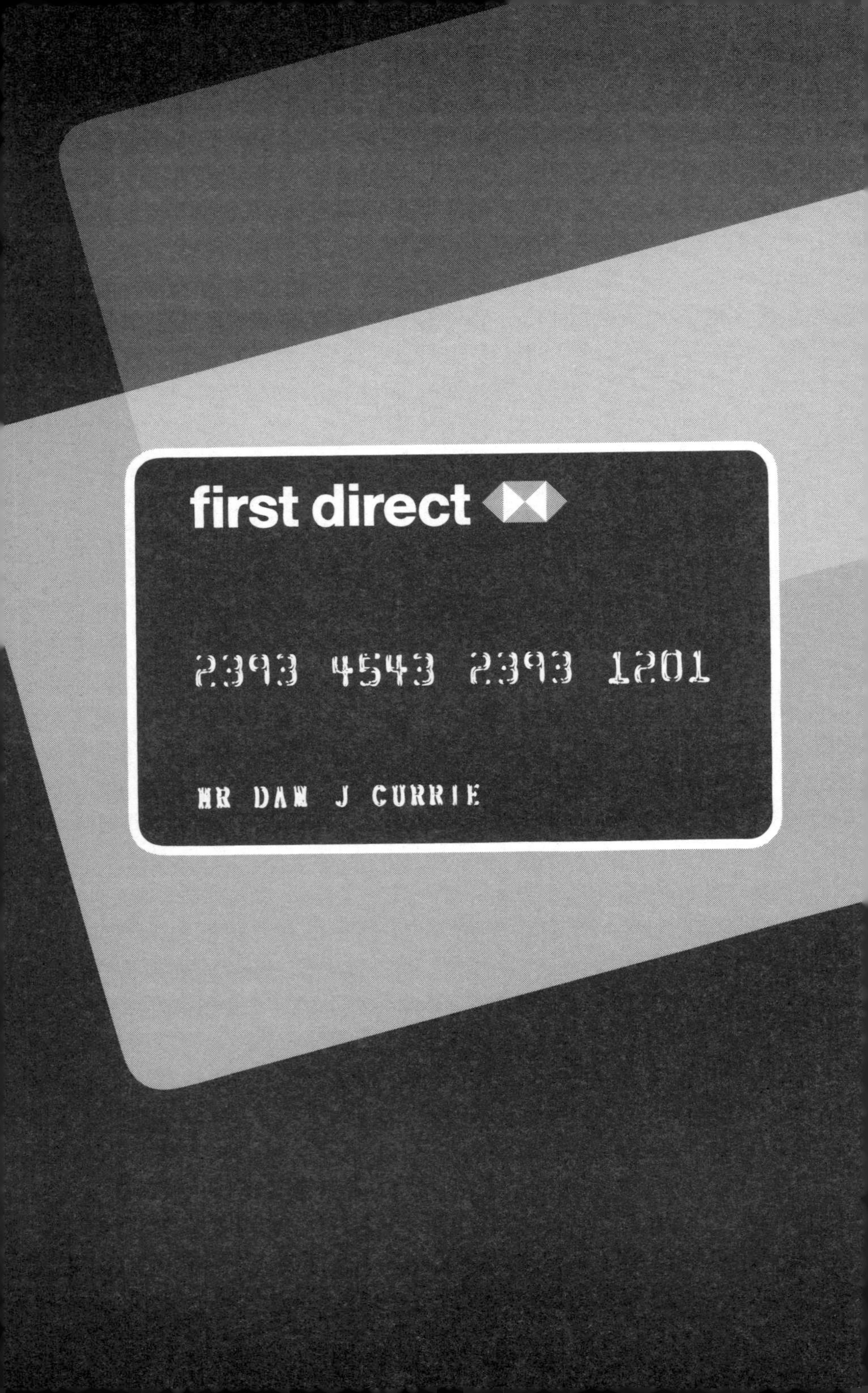
first direct
2393 4543 2393 1201
MR DAN J CURRIE

FEEL: EMPATHIZING WITH YOUR CUSTOMERS

CEOs can be human too. "It was just awful," said Tim Waterstone, the founder of Waterstone's, Europe's largest bookstore chain. He was talking about the state of book retailing in the mid-1980s, when stores would only stock best sellers and closed at midday on Saturdays. Tim has loved books all his life, but while going through a painful divorce he rediscovered how important they were for him. He took great pleasure in browsing in bookshops, but quickly realized that their limited stock, restricted opening hours, and unhelpful staff marred his enjoyment. He also realized that this presented an opportunity. "I reckoned that if I felt that way there must be several million out there like me."

The answer was the first Waterstone's bookshop, which opened in Old Brompton Road in London in 1982. By 2003 the company had grown to become the United Kingdom's leading specialist bookseller, with 200 high street locations across the United Kingdom, Ireland, and Europe. Waterstone's flagship store in Piccadilly is the biggest bookshop in Europe, comprising five floors of books, coffee bars, and even a restaurant.

Later, when recalling how he came to create the very successful Daisy & Tom department stores, Tim said, "I became cross with Mothercare [the children's retailer]. They have lost their vision." In fact, when shopping with his own small children and finding that he was forced to "drag them" from one store to another to obtain what they needed, he became so angry that he decided to create his own brand of children's department stores specializing in clothing, toys, and accessories. Daisy & Tom was started in 1997, and today there are five stores turning over £15 million. Tim has just acquired the Early Learning Centre chain, which will add 200 stores and £170 million turnover to his business.

Tim Waterstone is not alone. Many of the leading entrepreneurs today started their businesses because they were fed up with what was on offer. Sinclair Beecham and Julian Metcalfe started Pret A Manger when they despaired of the poor quality of sandwiches on offer near their offices in the City of London. Peter Boizot founded Pizza Express in 1965 because he was "fed up that he couldn't get a decent pizza in London." Ho Kwon Ping founded the Banyan Tree Hotels and Resorts because as a developer he reckoned he could make a better job of managing the hotel himself. He told us:

> Since no such resort existed at the time, we couldn't do a lot of market research. Instead it became a very personal thing .... We extrapolated from our own travels and holiday experiences, and we took it from there.

It would seem that passion has a place in successful business.

In the recession in the 1990s so many companies were downsizing, consolidating, or merging that executives spent their days worrying about cost-cutting, junk bonds, or management buy-outs. No wonder then that the bean counters rose to ascendance. This was the era of the CEO with an accounting background. There were some notable exceptions, of course, but nevertheless, whereas traditionally CEOs had come from the ranks of the engineers, sales, hoteliers, operations, or pilots – in other words the "doers" – now they were increasingly promoted from the "administrators."

Bob Ayling, CEO of British Airways in the late 1990s, had previously been BA's legal secretary. He was criticized for his lack of ability to engage with the customer-facing workforce, in contrast to his predecessor Sir Colin Marshall. Ayling was replaced by Rod Eddington, an airline man through and through and a consummate people person. That is not to say that he isn't numerate. He has led BA through very turbulent times and has restructured the cost base of the carrier, which regained its status as the most profitable airline in the world in 2005. Rod Eddington has very high levels of both IQ and what Daniel Goleman calls "EQ," or emotional intelligence. This is the ability to relate to situations at the emotional rather than the purely analytical level.

Focusing on operational efficiency is important of course. In the United Kingdom, during the 1980s and 1990s it was essential to overcome the endemic malaise of British industries: profit-losing, inefficient, unproductive organizations. The fact is that British business have learnt their lessons well. They have cut costs and become more efficient. Who would have predicted that Jaguar would be achieving better quality and customer satisfaction scores than all Japanese brands except Lexus in the JD Power customer satisfaction survey? But Six Sigma, ISO 9000, cost-cutting and re-engineering only gets you so far. The route to continued bottom-line growth has always been through increasing top-line revenues, not reducing costs. Even industries that are noted for their cut-throat pricing are focusing on revenues. O2, the mobile phone operator, invested heavily in upgrading its customer experience to drive top-line growth achieving a market-beating performance.[25] There is an old saying, "different strokes for different folks," and this is true for CEOs too. We think the pendulum in this decade will swing back to a more appropriate balance between scientific management and intuitive leadership; between hard and soft data; between IQ and EQ.

Harvard professor David McClelland's analysis of star performers in organizations found that the executives who demonstrated emotional intelligence (EQ) outperformed their targets by 15 to 20 percent; those who lacked it underperformed by almost 20 percent.[26]

Emotional intelligence is not just important for CEOs. Even nerds need it. Lyle Spencer Jr., director of research and technology at Hay/McBer, also carried out extensive research into the differences between average performers and stars. In his book *Working with Emotional Intelligence*[27] Daniel Goleman reported some of these results. One of the most surprising job arenas where emotional intelligence makes a competitive difference is computer programming, where the rate at which the top 10 percent exceed average performers in producing effective programs is 320 percent. And those rare superstars, in the top 1 percent of programmers, produce a boggling 1,272 percent more than the average. "It's not just computing skills that set apart the stars, but teamwork," Goleman commented. In other words the ability to relate to others emotionally is a greater predictor of success for programmers than computer skills.

We think there are three critical abilities for leaders who want to add "feel" to their repertoire:

- **Emote.** Don't be afraid to express or describe what you are feeling about a situation. It's what people do.
- **Engage.** Ask your customers or employees to express their feelings.
- **Empathize.** Close the gap between what you feel and they feel. Understand how similar and different what they feel is from what you feel.

These are abilities that Richard Branson has in abundance, and that have made him one of the most enduringly successful people in public life. For example, when he took over part of the old British Rail network and started Virgin Rail, Branson was shocked at what he found:

I remember going to a back room at Euston where the train drivers and people meet while they're waiting for their trains. It was the most despicable thing; British Rail had given them a horrible place, a hovel of a place. I decided to spend some money on giving them television to watch whilst they waited for the trains, games to play; again, treating people as human beings and encouraging them to keep in touch.[28]

In March 2007, Virgin Trains suffered a derailment of one of its high-speed overnight services. The crash was found to be as a result of faulty maintenance on the part of the track operator. Nevertheless, Branson, who was on vacation at the time, immediately flew back to the UK and was captured on film by TV crews at the site early the following morning talking to passengers and train crew. The image of Branson's drained face and dishevelled appearance conveyed that this was no public relations exercise but an emotional response to a terrible situation.

EMOTE

Don't be afraid to acknowledge or express what you are feeling about a situation. It's what people do.

The scientific school of management would have us believe that effective business executives are cool, calculating automatons, rather like the role of Gordon Gecko, played by Michael Douglas in the movie *Wall Street*. In fact the opposite is true. George Soros, the Hungarian investor who bets against national currencies and has amassed a fortune in the process, was asked how he knew when to cut his losses. He replied,

> *I feel the pain. I rely a great deal on animal instincts. When I was actively running the Fund, I suffered from backache. I used the onset of pain as a signal that there was something wrong with my portfolio.*[29]

This ability to emote brings a whole new source of data to executive decision making.

The world of marketing is predicated on persuading people emotionally to purchase a product or service. Consumers (and that includes you and us!) think emotionally, react emotionally, and express themselves emotionally. So if you really want to engage with consumers, remind yourself that you are one too, and engage with your own emotions. Think, for a minute, what makes a great political leader. Is it technical mastery of a set of political economic or social policies? Or is it the ability to connect with the hopes, fears, and aspirations of the people the individual seeks to lead? We may respect a politician who is intimately familiar with the economic principles of monetarism, but we believe in the politician who makes us feel that he or she knows what it is like to be "us."

So this ability to be in touch and express feeling holds true for political leaders too. As the choir sang hymns at his presidential inauguration, Bill Clinton cried. In fact it is said that Clinton often cried while in office, and yet he is considered to be one of the more intellectual US Presidents of the modern era. In this respect he was like President Reagan perhaps, who was known as "the Great Communicator." Reagan's training as an actor and ability to emote were demonstrated in an election debate with his opponent Walter Mondale. When Reagan smiled, people who watched him smiled too. When he frowned, so too did viewers. Mondale had no such emotional impact even among his political supporters, and went on to lose the election heavily. We do not advocate insincerity, but the point of the story was that Reagan used his skill to emote in a way that influenced the intellectual debate.

Martin Luther King, Winston Churchill, John F. Kennedy, Nelson Mandela, and Mahatma Gandhi were great leaders because they were passionate and cared deeply about making a difference in the world. Diana, Princess of Wales was probably the only member of the British monarchy in recent years to truly be loved by the public. This was in large part due to her active engagement with landmine and AIDS charities. The numerous photographs of her holding victims in her arms contributed to her public persona and the emotions she evoked in others. This was in stark contrast to the photographs the public usually sees of royalty: hands clasped firmly behind their backs, tweaking their cuffs or clutching handbags; anything in fact to avoid touching anybody.

This emphasis on feelings seems to be at odds with much that is taught on MBA courses. "If it can't be measured it can't be managed and therefore doesn't exist" is the philosophy. Facts, data and two-by-two grids all have their place, but are unlikely to inspire people to act. Feelings, on the other hand, are infectious. Tim Waterstone told us, "You have to understand the importance of the bottom line but everything we do is intuitive. People follow a dream, not a business plan." He went on to say that the biggest challenge he had had in his career is "finding financial directors who see their role as helping the organization achieve its vision rather than finding reasons why things should not be done."

Emoting is about being passionate, about making a difference, and then being ready to express it, and this applies to all types of business. Gordon Ramsay, the Michelin-star winning chef and successful entrepreneur, said:

> Some people ask me why I shout in the kitchen. They say that my leadership style is too full-on. The reason I lead this way is because I am passionate about what we do and about satisfying our customers. If one of my customers is waiting for something I'm going to say "Get that duck out to table 15 now," not, "When you have a moment would you kindly work on table 15's order." When customers are in the restaurant we are totally focused on them. The time to focus on each other is when the doors close.[30]

However, despite what people may believe, Gordon Ramsay is passionate about his people too. He just feels that the time to engage with his people is when he has the time to really listen to them.

We were at a conference recently and sat in the audience while Tom Peters gave one of his keynote addresses. In classic Tom Peters style he ranted, raved, and at times seemed on the verge of tears. Tom is a very intelligent man, but there are some speakers who are considered to be more academic, to have done more extensive research, or to have newer ideas. Yet Tom is considered to be the "*über guru*," or the guru of gurus, and audiences come back again and again to hear him deliver his message. Why? We think it is because he is passionate and emotes. He is the very antithesis of the dry academic consultant.

So the first guiding principle of Feel is simply to allow yourself to express and explore the very emotions that your customers have.

Ask your customers and your people to express their feelings.

In typical Gordon Ramsay style, the way he engages with people is "full on" too:

> I called a meeting with 35 of my managers and sommeliers and asked them, "What pisses you off when you come to work?" The results were extraordinary and we found out exactly what we needed to do in the business.[31]

Open engagement at this level is often missing in communications between managers and their staff. Philip Green, the billionaire retailer we discussed in the See chapter, is also keen to engage with his people, although perhaps not in quite the same way as Gordon Ramsay. He recently spent a full day calling each one of the 67 members of Arcadia's scholarship program to find out how they were getting on. With half of their course completed he thought he would get in touch personally.[32]

Some while ago, we were working with a large supermarket chain. At a conference of the top 2,000 executives the subject of communications was addressed, and members of the audience were invited to identify the worst examples of communication in the organization. Top of the list was the "regional manager visit." This is where the senior executive responsible for a region visits a store to discuss its performance. These typically had a damaging effect on staff morale, and sent the wrong message through the organization because the executive concerned usually only asked about "the numbers." He or she was often oblivious to taking people's time away from serving customers, and the focus was on looking for the things that were wrong rather than reinforcing what was right.

But how do you engage when you have large numbers of employees or customers? John Russell, managing director and VP of Harley-Davidson Europe, said, "The more you engage with people, the clearer things become, and the easier it is to see what you should be doing." That is why Harley executives are required to go out riding with their employees and customers on a regular basis. John went on to say:

If you move from being a commodity product to an emotional product, through to the real attachment and engagement that comes from creating a product experience, the degree of difference might appear to be quite small but the results are going to be much greater.[33]

KNOWING AND DOING: THE TESCO CLUBCARD

But what if you have millions of customers? Tesco, the United Kingdom's largest supermarket and the largest online grocer in the world, serves 12 million customers a week. Executives cannot engage with that many customers on a one-to-one basis; or can they? The Tesco Clubcard has 10 million members, and every time a customer uses the card a computer records when, where, what the customer bought, providing a record of his or her preferences and shopping habits. As a result Tesco is able to engage virtually with its customers and gain tremendous insight into their needs. This has enabled the firm to continually refine and personalize its offer to suit customer needs. It is almost impossible for any competitor to move in on an area covered by Tesco because the competitor cannot engage with the customers in the same way. Without this tremendous insight into the preferences of customers it becomes very difficult to create a more focused offer.

Tim Mason, Tesco's commercial director, talks about "knowing and doing" to describe this total focus on translating customer insight into customer value.[34] This in turn creates huge value for the organization, with the Clubcard producing more than £100 million in incremental sales each year. Tesco recently announced its results for its most successful year ever, reporting a profit of £2.5 billion for 2006. It earns £1 for every £8 spent by shoppers in Britain.

This result is in stark contrast to the findings of Gartner Research, which estimated that US$46 billion was spent on customer relationship management (CRM) systems in 2004, and yet 55 percent of CRM systems are reckoned to dilute earnings and drive customers away.[35] The reason for this is that the technology is used as a blunt instrument to "stalk" rather than "woo" customers. We think "CRM" really stands for Constantly Receiving Mailshots, because that is the reality that most customer experience as a result of this technology.

CRM systems are intelligent (high IQ) in their ability to handle vast amounts of data, but the way they are used all too often lacks any kind of empathy (EQ) with the needs of the customer. This attribute has to be designed in by the organizations that use them, and yet all too often the technology drives the customer experience rather than the other way around. Perhaps that is why Bearing Point found that despite the massive investment in CRM technology, 92 percent of financial services executives believe that there are still major opportunities to improve customer loyalty and growth.[36] It is interesting to note that Siebel, the market leader in CRM systems that are supposed to enable companies get closer to their customers, came last in a survey of customer satisfaction with technology companies' online services.[37]

One bank is flying in the face of conventional wisdom in the industry. While the four largest banks in Australia are busy closing branches, the Bank of Queensland has opened 38 new branches in Central Queensland and plans to open 100 more by 2006. It is now Australia's fastest growing bank and one of the country's top 150 listed companies. It has reported profits almost double those of just two years ago and has been voted Australia's Best Regional Bank for the past two years. So what is its secret for success? Engagement. It offers a "person2person™" service which reintroduces the notion of the bank manager and dealing with real people rather than IVR machines and call centers. Its motto is "Bank different."

Bank of Queensland operates an Owner-Managed Branch™ model whereby the manager runs the bank as a business. Peter Gibbons, the owner manager for the town of Grafton in New South Wales, said, "I grew up in the era of real bank managers and am a firm believer in the old-fashioned values of face-to-face service and going the extra mile for customers."

It would seem that it is not only customers who benefit from engagement. Students at the London Business School conducted a survey with 276 employees, and found that 41 percent of respondents reported that interaction with customers has the greatest impact on their energy at work. This compared with just 16 percent who are energized by their managers. There is a reason for this. In our book *Uncommon Practice*, we concluded that most executives are more likely to "stumble the mumble" than "walk the talk." In other words they are unclear in communicating what is really important, and rarely demonstrate it in their own interactions with employees.

Tom Peters encouraged a generation of leaders to "manage by wandering about." Many of the leaders we studied spend most of their time wandering around and talking with customers and employees to great effect, but this is the exception rather than the rule. The sad fact is that many of the leaders we see actually need guidance on how to do this effectively. Left to their own devices they will allow IQ to take over, and interrogate their poor unfortunate employees with a barrage of questions about the last period rather than actually connect at a human level. The *Uncommon Practice* leaders, however, have this rare ability to really engage and demonstrate through their personal behavior what is important. Stelios Haji-Ioannou, chairman of easyGroup, told us:

> *The first thing I did [when I started easyJet] was walk the talk; I took my tie off, started dressing down. I worked from an office in Luton. All of that was part of a plan to create a culture which keeps costs down.*

Engagement is a two-way process. Not only does it communicate what the leaders believe is important to the employees, but also creates a means to find out first-hand what is concerning them. But to really engage with people requires the ability to empathize.

EMPATHIZE

Close the gap between what you feel and how your customers or employees feel. Understand how similar and different what they feel is from what you feel.

In 1991 in an address to the Institute of Directors, Gerald Ratner, the chairman of a UK jewelry business with sales of £1.2 billion, made the mistake of describing one of his products, a sherry decanter, as "total crap." The press reported his remarks with glee, and it soon became headline news. His "jokey reference" cost Ratner his job, his personal fortune, and wiped an estimated £500 million off the company's value. What really damaged Ratner was his lack of sensitivity to the customers who bought his products thinking they were good value. In a moment of madness his lack of empathy with the feelings of his customers cost him his lifetime's work. But he is not alone. Even with the benefit of huge research and marketing budgets, organizations can get it spectacularly wrong.

BARCLAYS AND THE BIG MISTAKE

Barclays Bank aired a television advertisement called "Big idea" in 2001. It was a beautifully crafted ad featuring Anthony Hopkins as a "big shot" businessman, in his "big house", then being driven in his "big car" to a "big meeting." The tag line was "A big world needs a big bank." The ad was received with some acclaim by the industry, even receiving a bronze award at that year's British Television Advertising Awards, Unfortunately, Barclays customers said "Big deal!" The ad was criticized for reinforcing everything that is considered bad about the major banks: they don't care about the little person and are only interested in the big corporations and making as much money as they can. They are large, remote, and Big Brother-like.

To make matters worse, Matthew Barrett, Barclays' £3.2 million a year chief executive officer, was giving evidence to a Treasury Select Committee. Questioned by George Mudie MP about his attitudes towards personal finance, Barrett replied, "I do not bother with credit cards. It is too expensive. I have four young children. I give them advice not to pile up debts on their credit cards." Barclays is the United Kingdom's largest issuer of credit cards, and Barclaycard the best-known brand in the market, earning the bank £450 million profit each year. The banking profession was stunned by his remarks.

One competitor called it "a quite magnific[...]
never shake off."[38]

Contrast this with First Direct, the onli[...]
Research with 580,000 customers identi[...]
engage with a real person is an important [...]
customers. As a result First Direct's advertisi[...]
named "Call centers," which featured a custo[...] [...]g to camera
of her experience of calling First Direct and being able to speak to a
person to get help any time of the day or night. The simple
treatment, engaging message, and apparent empathy with how real
customers feel is estimated to have produced £3.8 in incremental
revenues for First Direct.

The difference between the Barclays and First Direct approaches is
reinforced by recent research by Forrester Group into what makes a
great brand.[39] The research was focused on the Australian market but
feels right intuitively for other markets too. The researchers found
that being "trustworthy" and "credible" were the two strongest
attributes of great brands, at 97 percent and 96 percent respectively,
while being "the biggest" was the least important, at just 15 percent.

Barclays' claim to be big did not strike a chord with customers, but
First Direct's use of a customer talking about actual experiences gave
credibility to its claim of being accessible. This example shows the
difference between "expectation marketing" and "experience
marketing." The former is when a company communicates a claim
that seeks to shape consumer expectations of what it is like to use its
products or services. It is the most common form of advertising.
The latter is when a company communicates actual customer
experiences in the form of an endorsement.

Of course the voice of the customer can work against you as HSBC
found out recently. The company that calls itself "the world's local
bank" decided to restrict a local branch in Dorset, England to only its
very wealthiest customers. The local public were outraged and the
story hit the national headlines.[40] What made it even worse was

BC spokesperson said, "We are trying to treat everyone
not everybody in the world is equal." The decision may
ll have been taken for very sound financial reasons. When looked
at from the distance of the boardroom, it may seem to be a logical
and rational thing to do, but when viewed from the customer
perspective it seems a decision driven by hubris and a stunning lack
of empathy. Ironically, HSBC owns First Direct suggesting that
empathizing with customers truly does become a major challenge
with organizational size.

COKE VERSUS PEPSI –
THE CLASSIC CHALLENGE

For example, while Coca-Cola was busy "Teaching the world to sing
in perfect harmony," Pepsi was holding the "Pepsi challenge" all over
the United States. Cola drinkers were invited to blind taste two colas.
One was Coke, the other Pepsi. In virtually every case consumers
picked the Pepsi sample as their favorite, and were surprised to learn
which one it was. The Pepsi challenge was aired extensively as a
television advertisement, and resulted in significant share gains for
Pepsi. So much so, that Coca-Cola was panicked into introducing
"New Coke" – which bombed. Emotional Coke customers formed
protest groups and lobbied to get their beloved beverage reinstated.
Finally Coke relented and "Classic Coke" was reintroduced.

So how did Pepsi manage to win the blind tasting test? Pepsi is
sweeter, and therefore in a sipping test will be preferred. Drink a can
of it, though, and Coke's sharper tang tends to be preferred. The
lesson from all of this is that engaging with customers, empathizing
with their feelings and marketing experiences rather than
expectations, results in more successful campaigns. Stelios Haji-
Ioannou, chairman of easyGroup, sums this up by saying," You can

spend £15 million on advertising, go bankrupt and your name can still mean nothing to people. Your brand is created out of customer contact and the experience your customers have of you."[41]

When we think of empathizing we tend to think of one-to-one situations, and of course, that is when empathy becomes most important. This is nowhere more so than in the doctor–patient relationship. Malcolm Gladwell in his book *Blink*[42] reports the work of medical researcher Wendy Levinson, who recorded hundreds of conversations between physicians and their patients. Approximately half of these doctors had been sued at least twice for medical malpractice. The other half had never been sued. The difference was not in their skills as surgeons but in their bedside manner. Levinson wanted to find out the differences in approach used by those doctors who had been sued and those who had not. What she found was fascinating. The surgeons who had never been sued spent more than three minutes longer with each patient (18.3 minutes versus 15 minutes). But more importantly, according to Gladwell:

> They were much more likely to make "orienteering" comments like "First I'll examine you, and then we will talk the problem over." They were more likely to engage in active listening, saying such things as "Go on, tell me more about that," and they were far more likely to laugh and be funny during the visit. Interestingly there was no difference in the amount or quality of information they gave their patients; they didn't provide more details about medication or the patient's condition. The difference was entirely in how they talked to their patients.

Gladwell goes on to relate an even more incredible piece of research, where recordings of doctor–patient conversations were made and then the actual words taken out using computers, leaving behind merely the tone of what was said and the inflections of voice. Now here is the amazing part. Independent judges were asked to listen to these slices of garbled recordings and rate them for qualities like warmth, hostility, and dominance. The judges knew nothing about the skill levels or experience of the surgeons, or what procedures they used. All they knew was the tone of voice being used; not even the words themselves. Yet the researchers were able to predict which doctors would be sued and which would not. In other words, the likelihood of getting sued as a doctor seems to be much more about lack of empathy than lack of medical ability.

LAWYERS ARE PEOPLE TOO!
CLIFFORD CHANCE AND ITS RAINMAKERS

Talking of being sued raises the issue of lawyers, and in particular what makes some lawyers "rainmakers," those who are top of their game in terms of finding, keeping, and sustaining relationships with clients. These highly successful rainmakers are so called because of their ability to keep revenues flowing into the firm at a level beyond the average partner. You would not think that there is much connection between these highly successful lawyers and the empathetic doctors that we have just spoken about; but there are some surprising similarities.

Shaun worked with Clifford Chance, the world's largest law firm, helping to develop client focus skills with partners worldwide. He conducted in-depth interviews with 20 senior partners in Asia, Europe, and the United Kingdom who are considered to be rainmakers in the firm. The purpose of the interviews was to find out these partners' backgrounds, influences, and approach to clients. Over 50 percent of the lawyers interviewed cited overseas or cross-cultural experience as being an important influencer in terms of how they approach client relationships. Early experiences working directly for clients (rather than through more senior lawyers) as well as secondments to client organizations were also considered important "shapers." These factors are important because they enable the lawyer to develop the interpersonal skills necessary to create strong working relationships with clients.

Stuart Popham, senior partner at Clifford Chance's London office, summed up the importance of the working relationship by saying:

> The experience of which lawyers (the client) likes are determined after working through the night with them ... if you are in one of these meeting rooms, and the pressure is on and you get the deal done or settle the case, whatever it is – you go away thinking "we did that together." There are other lawyers about whom the client would say, "I never want to spend another hour in that room with that man."

When rainmakers were asked to describe how they approached their work they spoke about:

- really listening to clients and responding to their issues
- demonstrating interest in and commitment to achieving results for clients
- showing that you are "part" of the client's team
- being prepared to be creative with the solution
- winning business through quality and relationships rather than price.

Stuart Popham summed up some of these activities by saying he felt successful lawyers were those that had made the transition through three levels of client service: "They move from being reactive to proactive to predictive." This last level is the ability to anticipate the client's requirements and provide the answer before clients even know they need one. In fact the difference between being a good lawyer and a trusted advisor is that a good lawyer is able to provide legal answers; a trusted advisor is able to help clients find legal solutions to their commercial or litigation problems. As Popham says, "Define a great lawyer; is it someone who knows the law or someone who can apply the law?"

This is the essence of See, Feel, Think, Do. The successful business leaders we spoke to were constantly looking for opportunities to make a difference for their customers rather than waiting for customers to ask, or worse still, research or business results to reveal there was a problem. The ability to be empathetic is as important as the ability to be analytic, yet is rarely taught in law school or business school.

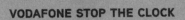

VODAFONE STOP THE CLOCK

Vodafone is the world's largest cellular phone network operator and the dominant player in many of the markets in which it operates. The Vodafone brand is recognized around the world, and yet Vodafone, along with most of its competitors, does not evoke much public affection. The network operators are generally thought to be expensive, bureaucratic in their dealings with customers, and lacking any kind of empathy. That may be about to change.

Vodafone has been under pressure from aggressive price cutting in the market. Each operator seeks to offer better discounts and a lower tariff than the others, and new entrants like the easyGroup are coming into the market with heavily price-driven promotions. But as Tim Yates, chief marketing officer at Vodafone UK, told us:

The focus in the industry has been on the rational elements of pricing. The belief has been that if you reduce your prices you change people's behavior in your favor. In fact we believe that mobile phone usage is much more of an emotional event, and that to change customer behavior you first have to change the customers' attitude.

Vodafone's premium position and core expertise in "understanding mobility" led it to engage with customers to really understand their attitudes to using their mobile phone. What Vodafone found was that customers didn't understand the tariff they were on, considered calls to be expensive, and thought that they were speaking on their phone for longer than they actually were. In fact Julian Bessey (senior product manager) and his team found that the average call length was only two minutes. As a result of these perceptions, customers make two-thirds of their calls over land lines, and only one-third on their mobiles, reserving their longer conversations with friends and family for the evenings and weekends, when they can call from their home phone. The Vodafone team realized that in order to change customer behavior while staying true to the vision of enabling mobility, a new approach was required. Simple price cutting would not be sufficient.

The breakthrough came when the team really tried to empathize with customers and decided actually to observe how they were using the phones. How were they feeling? What would it take for them to use their mobile phone for longer calls? What constrained them? They observed customers making calls, and as they listened to customer conversations, they realized that customers were constantly thinking, "How much is this call costing me?" As a result customers would say, "I'll make this brief because I'm speaking from my mobile."

The team decided to try a test promotion whereby customers would be offered free calls at weekends to encourage them to use their phone for all their calls. The results were astounding. Not only did customers take up the offer, but their value increased by over 10 percent per month due to higher usage during the week as well.

In May 2005 Vodafone launched its "Stop the Clock" initiative. It allows customers to speak up to 60 minutes but pay for only three, at evenings and weekends when longer calls were generally made on a fixed-line phone. The idea was to liberate customers from the pressure of needing to minimize their mobile phone usage, and encourage them to use their phone to achieve more from life. As the advert says, "Sometimes life's more than a three-minute conversation." In an industry noted for its small print and exclusions, Stop the Clock aimed to present a big idea uncluttered with conditions.

When the idea was trialed with customers they asked, "What's the catch?" The answer was, "There isn't one," and so that is what Vodafone also put into its advertisements.

The Stop the Clock story illustrates the importance of being able to See, Feel, and then Think. The initiative required a very complex business case to be made, that was estimated to have been likely to have an impact on revenues of millions of pounds if Tim and his team had done their sums wrong. Now those are the sort of figures that would make anyone stop to think – and "Think" is our next chapter.

5

THINK: THERE'S NO SUCH THING AS A STUPID IDEA

It started with a simple idea that Jeff Bezos had. The average bookstore has about 150,000 titles in stock at any one time; a really big one maybe has an inventory of up to 300,000. "Why can't we have a million?" asked Jeff Bezos. "Because," said the experts, "sourcing that amount of stock will bankrupt you." Well, Bezos asked the question, didn't like the answer the experts gave him, and went out and got the million titles. As he admitted later, "Those people who told us it would nearly kill us were right. It nearly did." But Amazon's ability to offer almost any book that anyone wanted became the phenomenon that drove its brand success.

THINKING THE UNTHINKABLE
AMAZON AND ONE CLICK

Amazon often thinks the unthinkable. For example, take one-click shopping. Until the arrival of Amazon, retail on the web was defined by the shopping cart approach. Basically, online retailers simply simulated the real-world experience of visiting a store, where you fill up your trolley, shopping basket, or hands by browsing aisles/sections and selecting groceries, gifts, books, and so on. So on the web you clicked on a shopping cart icon and scrolled up and down and in and out of sections, choosing what you wanted and adding it to your cart.

There was a big problem with this: it took too long! People expected the Internet to deliver a speedy service that was not a simulation of real life; they wanted an experience that could only be found online. They were not comparing the time it takes to go online, browse, shop, and purchase with the time it takes to get into a car, drive to a supermarket, shop, and queue at the checkout. They were comparing it with an "expectation" they had of how fast and easy it should be, and with the other form of home shopping: phoning. People were abandoning their online carts, often halfway through the shopping process, and not making purchases because of frustration at the length of time the process took. It could often take longer, for example, to buy cinema tickets online than by phone.

Why was this, Jeff Bezos and his team at Amazon asked? Why were online retailers just replicating the real-life shopping experience in a virtual environment? Put simply, it was because online retailers were not thinking that what people wanted in the virtual world was a totally different experience, not a carbon copy of reality.

Amazon dared to ask what many might have thought a stupid question: can't we just get the shopping done with one click of a button? And it realized that actually you just about could. Amazon realized you could store "cookies" to capture all the buyer info (such as the shipping address and credit card info), and in future the purchaser would only need to press one button to buy. It spent thousands of hours and millions of dollars developing this "cookie" technology, which it then patented in the United States. It is a simple concept that has revolutionized home shopping.

Amazon's patenting of the technology was the source of much controversy. People objected to the fact that Amazon benefited from other people's early web development, and they complained that Amazon should not try to hog advantages like this. Jeff Bezos thought about this, and his response was to write an open letter about it on the Amazon website. He explained that the patent was valid not necessarily for the technology alone, which is trivial to duplicate, but for the breakthrough thinking.

Thinking. That word is the most important in the process we are describing here. And it is what Amazon and others who develop great ideas do a lot. They think. They think for themselves. They interrogate what is the given, the norm, and they think how it can be changed. They don't accept the received wisdom of others or the findings of market research and consultants' reports. They question;

they ponder; they are possessed of a restless curiosity that pushes them towards discovery and insight. The capacity for independent thought, the ability to "reason," are the most powerful gifts we have as humans, and among our greatest responsibilities. So why is it when we go to work that we so often seem to throw that gift away and delegate that responsibility to others?

Amazon thinks. Apple thinks different. When IBM was founded over one hundred years ago, its corporate mantra was: Think.

How, then, do we break down the stages of "thinking" to help us understand and improve the experiences of our customers? We have identified three guiding principles:

- **Cause and effect.** Interrogate like a child why things are the way they are. Be naïve in questioning what factors are affecting the moment that your customer experiences your brand.
- **Perfect world.** Think outside of the box. What is the perfect experience that we can bring customers?
- **"Why?" and "Why not?"** Challenge how this would bring you and your customer real value, and challenge why it can't be done.

Let's take them one at a time:

CAUSE AND EFFECT

Interrogate like a child why things are the way they are. Be naïve in questioning what factors are affecting the moment that your customer experiences your brand.

Let us give you a short story of how this principle works in a real-life situation. A few years ago a public transport system in a major city experienced a series of delays in the morning rush hour during weekdays. It discovered that the principal reason for the delays was that trains were having to stop because a passenger had fallen ill on the train and had to receive medical care. The trains lacked modern conveniences, especially air conditioning, which made them hot, stuffy, and over-crowded: exactly the kind of conditions that can induce fainting in certain types of people. The train operator had stacks of data about the running of its trains, and it was able to identify that the majority of the people who were falling ill at rush hour on the train in the morning were women. It also knew that the women were in a certain age bracket, and it also knew that most of them were on their way to work. What it couldn't work out was why the illnesses happened.

That insight came from a female station assistant. As a woman herself who worked, often on an early shift, she understood exactly what happened to those women that was causing them to faint. They were busy, they were rushing to get up and get out the door to get to work on time, and they might even have had to feed their kids before going. What they weren't doing, she sensed, was very simple: they were not having their breakfast. She told her bosses what she thought, and subsequent research confirmed that that was indeed what these passengers had in common: they were boarding a hot, stuffy, overcrowded train when their blood sugar was low.

Simple. But the great thing is what the transport operators did next. They did a deal with a maker of breakfast cereals that wanted to promote its new "breakfast bar" – positioned as breakfast on the go for people on the go. These were handed out at stations, specifically to women. It encouraged those women to remember that breakfast was needed, and of course, the benefit to the company was reminding consumers that a solution to their breakfast needs was available.

Too often we only think of our customers as having lives when they are in our stores or using our product. We don't think enough about what might be shaping their attitudes or behavior toward our brand before they come through the doors. A few years ago, airlines only thought about the experience on the plane as defining the customer experience; then they began to think about check-in and waiting time. (They introduced lounges to help relax and pamper business people, for example.) It took someone like Richard Branson to take this even further: he realized that the stress of a journey begins when the passenger is leaving home or work for the flight, not when he or she gets to the airport. "Will my taxi turn up? Will the train be on time? Will the traffic be bad? And if I am delayed how will I let the airline know?" These are the questions nagging away at the traveler. Branson asked himself why people thought like this. The answer was simply because at the point that passengers are leaving their house or work, they are remote from the airline. So Branson introduced the concept of limousines and limo bikes to pick up passengers at their home and work, and even "drive through" check-ins so that passengers would not have to worry about queuing at counters. He was thinking about cause and effect.

PERFECT WORLD

Think outside of the box. What is the perfect experience that we can bring customers?

"We basically have a very child-like dream, really," said Charles Dunstone, CEO of The Carphone Warehouse. "We absolutely, fervently believe that if you have to buy a mobile phone, there is nowhere better, no organization that will care more about it than we do ... and until everyone buys their phone from The Carphone Warehouse, we won't really give up."

What Dunstone's words reveal is the relentless pursuit of perfection that is needed to ensure that customers come to his stores. It is not good enough to have had a great concept, or an excellent launch, or a good year; the pursuit of the perfect experience requires a continual consideration of what is working and what could be done better. And it also involves a continuous dialog with customers to understand what they value and would want more of. For example, following the unprecedented demand for its TalkTalk product, Dunstone's December 2006 blog entry read, "Our focus for the year ahead is to rebuild people's confidence in our product and in our ability to deliver it." Knowing Charles Dunstone that is exactly what he will do.

**APPLE AND THE iPOD:
A PERFECT MUSICAL WORLD**

Take Apple Computers, for instance. Apple has remained one of the enduring brand success stories of the last 30 years because it has repeatedly thought differently, and dared to think about the perfect experience it could bring its customers. It famously launched its Apple Macintosh computers in 1984 with a spectacular advert – broadcast during the Superbowl, just about the most expensive media slot there is – showing an Orwellian world of people enslaved to mainframe computing. Through this grim servility runs a woman who throws a hammer through a huge television screen showing Big Brother's face. It was an iconic moment in advertising, and communicated Apple's child-like quest for the perfect customer experience: in this case, liberating human creativity through computing.

Apple has endured its share of ups and downs in its time, and there was undoubtedly a moment in the early 1990s, after Steve Jobs had left and when it began to formalize and co-brand initiatives with IBM, that many feared it had lost its way. However, the return of Steve Jobs in 1998 heralded a return of the brand to its creative roots, and a rediscovery of its corporate soul: a challenging, restlessly inquiring spirit that sought to liberate human creativity through easy to use, esthetically beautiful technological products, or "human tools" as they have been described. The iMac with its colorful range of Internet-enabled computers and the G-Mac are examples of that spirit – as is the iPod.

The iPod is an excellent example of someone thinking differently, of imagining what the perfect customer experience would be, and making it happen. iPod is not an entirely new product concept. Other hard-drive-based music players existed before. MP3 players had in fact been all the rage amongst a select group of tech-savvy types, people particularly in the creative industry who spend far more time working at their computers than is healthy. But why had this concept not been embraced by a wider audience?

Tony Fadell was a product designer who conceived the original idea for what would become the iPod. He had realized that there were two problems with existing MP3 players that made them difficult to use. It took too long to load up music and download it onto the MP3 player, and they took up too much space. Why did this need to be so? He devised a system which used a high-speed FireWire interface to transfer files, and a tiny hard drive that would make the device a fraction of the size of similar products. However, Fadell found it hard to get backing for his device. He had met both Philips and RealNetworks before Apple employed him as an independent contractor to make the idea work. Apple shared Fadell's simple thinking – why couldn't people carry all their favorite music around with them in one device? Why did we need to carry a case load of CDs around with us if we wanted to hear more than one or two albums?

Apple took the idea of thinking differently further with the iPod – it designed it not just as an easy to carry digital music player but as a thing of beauty. The casing was beautiful: clean, white with soft edges that echo the shape of the Apple logo. It was so small it could fit easily into a jacket or trouser pocket, encouraging people to take it with them wherever they went. Then there were the ear buds. Almost every set of speakers for MP3 players, CD players, or personal stereos had black or gray ear buds. Apple made its white to fit the dominant color of the brand, demonstrating its commitment to an esthetic that would be intrinsic to the brand, but above all showed the company's constant devotion to thinking about every part of the customer experience.

In fact the story of the iPod is one of a continuous quest to improve the customer experience, the pursuit of perfection, if you will. Every few months, it seems a new upgrade, a new feature, or a new accessory is introduced, always either in response to or anticipating customer needs. When the iPod was launched in 2001, the one main disadvantage it had was that it was very expensive (US$400). A product that was designed to be easy to use by everyone and everywhere was too expensive for many. But within one year, Apple had launched two new upgrades (a 10 gigabyte (GB) and a 20GB version). The arrival of the 20GB version was accompanied by a price cut in the 10GB and original 5GB versions, making iPods more affordable for many.

Apple did not stop there; the iPod Mini and the iPod Shuffle have also been launched, again offering the iPod brand at a more sensitive price for millions of people. Apart from introducing a portfolio of different price points, Apple constantly introduced other ideas to enhance the user experience. At the start of 2003 it announced the option of special edition iPods which would carry a customer's requested favorite graphic symbol or text (including signatures by famous music stars such as Madonna) on the casing. Later that year, responding to concerns that only people who had Apple computers could get the Apple iPod, the company released a new version of the product which was not only even smaller but came with a connector that could interface with both a FireWire and a USB2.0 port for PCs.

By the end of 2003 customers were beginning to complain about the battery life, noticing that the battery on their original iPod was not delivering the promised running time. Apple responded by replacing the battery of affected iPods either for free if they were under warranty or for US$99 if they were out of warranty. Further improvements were made over time: reducing the amount of space that the scrolling wheel took up, redesigning the ear buds to reduce background noise, introducing a color slide show player to accompany music tracks. However one of the most important innovations for customers was not in the hardware but in the software: the introduction of iTunes, Apple's online music library, which allowed users not only to store their own tracks, copied from CDs, but to "buy," download, and store music online. iTunes came with a feature which when online, instantly recognized the tracks which had been copied from the users' CDs into the library and automatically "tagged" them (listing the details of each track: title name, singer, time, and so on) and also finding the copy of the original album cover online and storing that too.

Throughout the development of the iPod's life, Apple has relentlessly thought about the minutiae of the customer experience, and with a child-like enthusiasm has created features which enhance the users' enjoyment and sense of control. The results have been phenomenal. By September 2003 (two years after launch) Apple had sold 1.4 million iPods. In June 2005 (less than two years later) it had sold over 14 million, including 5.3 million in the first quarter of 2005 alone. And that does not include the burgeoning accessories market, the sales of iTunes, and so on.

As well as the impressive sales performance, the iPod has become a celebrity icon and an added-value accessory: BMW cars introduced a special iPod interface so that the machine could play through the in-car speakers and be operated through the stereo; the Mori Art Museum in Tokyo used iPods for its guided audio tour, and the rock group U2 was used on a special edition of the iPod (in all-black with a red scroll) with a digital boxed set of its music in November 2003.

SONY AND HOW TO PLAY THE GAME

Sony Playstation is another example of a company thinking continuously about how it can create the perfect experience for its customers. Here, Sony is helped by the fact that since what it sells is a virtual game, the possibilities are limitless. The Playstation's rise to pre-eminence has not been a smooth ride. In fact it was almost stillborn. Originally Sony's intention was to develop a games console in conjunction with Nintendo, which in the early 1990s dominated the computer games marketplace together with Sega. It was only when Nintendo twice pulled out of a deal with Sony to co-produce the games console that Sony decided, in 1992, to go it alone. That was a daunting task. The company had no games heritage at the time, being a consumer electronics brand rather than a computer games brand; it had no presence in the arcade market which drove brand recognition and facilitated customer trial and word of mouth recommendation, and it had no in-house development team. But Sony did have two things going for it: a great marketing expertise, and the determination (and financial muscle) to push its product.

One thing that Sony learnt very quickly was that the user experience needed to constantly challenge and inspire, and seem as near "realistic" within the parameters of a fantasy world as was possible. Technology would move quickly, and people's expectations would keep increasing. Therefore Sony had to produce something extraordinary, a "wow" factor each time it launched a product, otherwise there would be no compelling reason to buy. Moreover it understood that the beauty of this market is that you could demonstrate this "wow" factor in a very visual way.

When the world saw the first Playstation, the "hardware" looked unexceptional (no different from a conventional PC). It was the on-screen demonstration that captured the imagination. A "lifelike" dinosaur head was shown on screen, and then merely through the use of a joystick was manipulated. The effect was so realistic that it made users feel as though they had control over a version of reality. They had the power of Playstation in their hands.

Right at the beginning, the Playstation established that it had the "product" to deliver an exceptional experience. However what has really fueled the Playstation's growth to its position as the number one games brand worldwide has been the way it has put the customers' feelings when experiencing the game at the center of its marketing. And much of this has been by the power of observation. In the United Kingdom for instance, Sony noticed that the concept of power that lay behind the Playstation brand had a particular significance for its primary audience, teenage gamers. They were at an age where they wished to rebel against or at least subvert parental authority, where they wanted to be liberated from the rules and disciplines of the home.

The Playstation gave them a powerful release into a world of their own. Recognizing this, Sony ran an inspired advertising campaign in 1996. Instead of advertising a new product, a new game, or a new feature, Sony came up with the idea of a Society Against Playstation. Geek-looking wholesome parents would be the spokespeople of the adverts, talking about clean living and healthy imaginative play, and only at the end, in an almost whisper, would they warn parents against the dangers of Playstation.

The idea of running an advert which 99 percent of the time did not mention the brand, and for the 1 percent when it did was advising people not to buy it, might seem like a "risky" idea, but it was entirely in sync with the target audience's mindset: the subversive sense of power that Playstation gave to users. Sony even took the idea into the in-store experience, creating a "forbidden zone" around its products, with notices telling people that they should not play the Playstation game. This fun and challenging approach worked wonders for the brand. Six months after launch, sales had tripled in the United Kingdom.

This reinvention of product and the marketing focus on the extraordinary feeling that customers should experience have continued right through to today. The tone of the advertising campaign changed from the satirical Society Against Playstation to a more epic and brooding "secret lives" theme – where users are featured talking to camera about the fantasy lives they lead through the power of Playstation. Again, there was little demonstration of product; instead there was an almost mesmeric concentration on the emotional experience of the consumers.

One of the best-known features of the Playstation is the symbols used for operating the game. The way that Sony used this in its marketing stemmed from its observation of both the consumer experience and the consumer emotion. The symbols were originally chosen to help differentiate Sony's joystick. These symbols also lent themselves to graffiti, or the kind of scrawling on schoolbooks that children, especially teenagers, enjoy. The symbols became a form of secret language, another manifestation of the power that Playstation confers on its users. Sony began to use this in communications, eventually producing a ground-breaking campaign where the four symbols were discovered (almost like Close Encounters of the Third Kind) in everyday surroundings. Accidentally arranged by someone into a particular pattern, they would unleash a transforming force.

The economic power of Playstation for Sony was enormous. By 1999, (according to the BBC's website) it was making more money for the company than all its other consumer electronics products combined, and had sold more than 50 million units worldwide – a staggering achievement within five years of launch, particularly for a company with no games heritage when it launched its first product. Today, Playstation continues to be the number one brand worldwide despite increasingly hot competition from Nintendo and Microsoft, and even from new entrants like Nokia.

The point of this story is that Sony realized that the perfect customer experience was about the power of fantasy, and that in such a situation, the way the product was marketed and advertised was as much part of that experience as the product itself. The company observed and listened to its consumers carefully, and responded with campaigns that talked directly to their emotions and dreams. It chose unusual and unconventional approaches to connect with them. Rarely has the communications of a product been such a perfect part of the customer experience.

WHY AND WHY NOT?

Challenge why this would bring you and your customer real value, and challenge why it can't be done.

The iPod and the Playstation are both also examples of companies constantly asking itself what value they can bring to their customers and interrogating why something can't be done. Increasingly today, companies and the people who work for them need to challenge the way things are done. It is a feature of our increasingly dynamic, fragmented, demanding, and experience-hungry society that people want more and for less money and time. Look at something as simple as non-alcoholic drinks. Twenty years ago, there were fizzy drinks and fruit juices. Now we have waters (still, sparkling, flavored, and vitamin enriched), fruit juices, fruit blends, fruit smoothies, fizzy drinks for sport, fizzy drinks for health, fizzy drinks for fun, fizzy drinks for ... well, you get the picture. We are (excuse the pun) saturated with drinks. You might not think this is a market where anyone could offer something new. But a company called Innocent Drinks thought differently.

Innocent Drinks is a UK-based company which specializes in fruit smoothie drinks made with all pure ingredients and only fruit. Like Pret A Manger, its founders were people who simply couldn't find the product they were looking for, and so decided to make it themselves. Like Tim Waterstone, they hoped there were a million others like themselves.

Richard Reed and two friends from college had been looking for a business they could set up and run themselves. One of their spare-time hobbies was making fruit smoothies – well, not a hobby, more a party trick. They would make the smoothies from pure fruit only, and their friends were highly appreciative. Richard and his friends made their own smoothies because they couldn't find a smoothie on the market that they liked: the products had either artificial ingredients which undermined the purity of the product, or natural additives such as sugar which affected the taste.

Having received such rave reviews from friends, Reed and his friends decided to see if there could be a wider market for their product. The research method they chose to understand what potential there could be was a brilliant example of See, Feel, Think, Do research. They turned up at a music festival (where they reckoned they would find the kind of people who would be interested in such a product – that is, people like themselves), and pitched their stall selling their own pure fruit smoothies. In front of the stall they placed two big bins for empty cups, and in front of the bins they placed a sign which read, "If you think we should give up our day jobs and make these smoothies for a living, then place your empties in this bin. If you don't, place them in the other one." At the end of the day, the "yes" bin was crammed to overflowing, and a business was born.

There will be management consultants and MBA professors who will be horrified at the appallingly slipshod and unscientific research method that Innocent used to convince itself that there was a business case for its brand. However, those of us who live in the real world will see that what the friends did was clever. They instinctively sought out a place where their target market could be found in significant quantities, to observe in a real-life setting and on a quantifiable basis (number of empties in the yes bin) reactions and potential demand to a proposed product. No focus groups here!

What Innocent showed in its marketing research was a simple, honest, uncomplicated, but highly clever and cost-effective approach. It was a refreshing, almost naïve – in fact one could say, innocent – approach. This approach has also informed all the company's marketing efforts. The product is pure fruit and nothing added: no sugar, no colorings, nothing. The packaging and promotions are witty but straightforward. The ingredients lists simply give the name of the fruit, such as strawberry or blueberry. They do not over-hype the names in a Ben-and-Jerry style of super-cool marketing – there's no "rocking raspberry" or "guzzleholic grapefruit." Innocent have fun, though. For example among the bland statement of ingredients will be something unusual like "a few pebbles,'" and at the end of the ingredients list is a note, "'We lied about the pebbles."

Here is a great example of how the Innocent approach to marketing translates into reality. It shows the importance that tone of voice has for the company, and the importance of hiring the right people with the right instinct. A colleague of ours, Max, bought an Innocent Smoothie from a shop and on tasting it noticed it was fizzy. He left it out on his desk instead of throwing it away, and bam!, it exploded all over his desk. He wrote to Innocent explaining what had happened. Here is the response. It is a brilliant example of how to use your intuition to deal with a customer complaint and get it right.

From: Erin's Little Helper [mailto:tempmarketing@innocentdrinks.co.uk]
To: Max
Subject: RE: exploding drinks

Hi Max,

Thanks very much for your funny email but big apologies for your unfortunate innocent experience. What a very badly behaved smoothie that was – I hate to think what influences it picked up after it left the pastoral haven that is our factory and made its way to the big bad world of chiller shelves. Just to explain what probably happened to this one: as you no doubt know our drinks are 100% fresh, natural and rather gorgeously lovely. As they don't contain any nasty preservatives or other gunk they need to be treated very carefully by being chilled at 0–5°C (as it says on our labels and on all the boxes we send them out in). If, somewhere along the chiller chain, they don't get treated with the TLC they deserve they may start to get warm, start to ferment and go fizzy. This is a totally natural process and won't be harmful at all – it just doesn't taste very nice. (Unless you like fizzy fruit, of course.) The fact that it was then left under your desk to ferment even more freely explains its attempts to repaint its local environment. Hmmm, bet your office cleaners now wish they'd done a more thorough job of emptying the bins... I hope the office looks a lot more cheery now, very Jackson Pollock.

We'd love to send you a case of our finest drinks as an apology. Please could you send in your <u>daytime</u> address, postcode and contact phone number of where someone will be in to sign for the drinks and pop them in the fridge. As I won't be back in the office for a couple of weeks, please could you send the details to <u>erin@innocentdrinks.co.uk</u> Please could you also let us know where you bought the drink, what recipe it was and – if possible – what the enjoy by date was on the bottle, also any other letters or numbers stamped onto the bottle. Thanks.

With best wishes,

Lucinda
(Erin's helper)

Max was delighted with the response and has sent this email around to as many people as he can – the power of customer advocacy! How many companies would have let such an informal and amusing customer response out of their door? Innocent has an instinctive feel for what is and what is not right.

Innocent entered an extremely competitive and fragmented marketplace and within seven short years has not only carved out a distinctive niche, but has built a successful business. This year it is forecasting sales in excess of £100 million, and is selling over 2 million smoothies a week. That's not bad for a company whose market research investment was £500 on fruit and a couple of tickets to a music festival.

If Innocent Drinks might seem like a quirky example of British eccentricity in a market sector where consumers expect new and interesting ideas, then let us look across the Atlantic and to a market sector where consumers have low levels of interest, and see how asking simple but profoundly challenging questions can transform expectations and responses to a company.

PROGRESSIVE INSURANCE: TAKING THE STRESS OUT OF CUSTOMERS' LIVES

Progressive is the third-largest motor insurance company in the United States, and has averaged a jaw-dropping 75 percent annual profit increase since 2001. The company has grown successful on the back of the management asking some powerful questions.

Shortly after taking up his first job with Progressive, former CEO Peter Lewis was attending a management meeting one day when one of the underwriters complained about independent agents who tried to persuade him to cover "non-standard" customers; in other words, high-risk drivers who had been turned down by other insurance companies. Lewis spoke up. "They're bringing us potential business. Can't we find a way to write these people?" This question led Progressive to becoming more and more focused on the high-risk niche, and seeing its premiums soar. Lewis had identified a niche that no one else wanted, and Progressive grew rapidly on the back of it.

Some years later, in 1988, California passed Proposition 103, a referendum to regulate auto insurance and reduce escalating premiums. Nearly 20 percent of Progressive's business was written in California, and this cost the company US$60 million in refunds. Lewis called it "the most frustrating experience" of his career, and because the legislation nearly put his company out of business he got really mad. But at the same time it caused him to evaluate the way the company was doing business. So he went to Washington and met with representatives from a number of consumer groups. He asked them this question, "What's wrong with auto insurance?" They told him that it was not competitive and lacked credibility. So Lewis decided to do something about it. He started what the company calls "information transparency," which means that the company quotes Progressive's rates to consumers along with the rates of its competitors – even when those rates are cheaper. This policy of transparency, and the trust that it created in the brand, changed the way that the company is viewed.

It was a personal tragedy that led to Peter Lewis's most successful initiative. In 1952, his elder brother was killed in a car accident. This tragic experience had a profound effect on Lewis. He says that it:

> ... makes every car accident an emotional experience for me. I can't take them lightly. We're not in the business of auto insurance. We're in the business of reducing human trauma and economic costs of automobile accidents – in effective and profitable ways.

These deep feelings led Lewis to asking the question, "Why can't we reduce the trauma of an accident for our customers in a way that is also profitable for us?" That question led to the management team brainstorming different approaches until they hit upon the idea of on-the-spot claims assessment. Progressive has transformed the customer experience, and in so doing differentiated itself from every other motor insurance company.

Today Progressive has a fleet of over 3,000 immediate response vehicles (IRVs) nationwide, each fitted with laptop computers, intelligent software, and wireless access to the Internet. The company receives about 25,000 calls a day, and when those calls are from customers who have had an accident, they are routed to claims representatives who initiate an immediate response in a matter of minutes. The IVR, driven by a mobile claims assessor, races to the scene of the accident, often arriving before the police or emergency services. Lewis says that these assessors are designed to help the customer's "emotional EKG" by sorting out all the stressful details at the point that the customer needs the most help.

The interesting by-product of this is that the company saves money as well. Because vehicles get inspected straight away, they get repaired sooner, which means less storage and rental car costs. Because the reps are out dealing with customers rather than pushing paperwork, they are more productive, and Progressive requires fewer assessors. Because the company provides instant help, the customers are much less likely to get mad at the other driver, and start legal proceedings which cost the insurers money. And finally, because the damage is assessed first-hand the company is much less likely to get stung by over-inflated damage quotes from repair shops. The result is less stress for customers, a highly differentiated experience, and greater speed. This leads to lower costs, which are in turn fed back in the form of lower premiums, making Progressive even more price competitive.

Progressive's new CEO, Glenn Renwick, is continuing the tradition of using the power of "Why?". His most recent innovation has been the introduction of a concierge service, which is now available across 18 metropolitan areas. Clients bring in their damaged cars for repair, and are given a hire car and a beeper.

Progressive organizes all of the activities required to repair the car, and notifies the customer when it is ready. In 2005, *Forbes* magazine named Progressive as one of the best-managed companies in America, and the top-ranked insurance company.

This readiness to keep asking "Why?" and "Why not?", and to make fundamental changes to the customer experience as a result of answering those questions, also helps to keep Progressive ahead of its rivals. It routinely asks customers a number of questions including:

1 In general, how satisfied are you with Progressive as your auto insurance provider?
2 How likely are you to refer someone to Progressive?

Over 89 percent of customers are satisfied with Progressive, and 74 percent are extremely satisfied. We ask these same questions when we conduct our Customer Experience Management +™ [43] survey with our clients, and Progressive's results are among the highest we have seen.

Amazon, Apple, Sony Playstation, Progressive, The Carphone Warehouse, and the many other companies we have featured so far in this book dare to think, and to think differently. But they don't just think differently; they go further. They have the courage of their convictions and make it happen. In other words they dare to do.

6

DO:
MAKE IT SO

"Make it so," says Captain Jean-Luc Picard of the *Starship Enterprise* at the end of every episode of *Star Trek: The Next Generation*. If only execution was as easy in real life as in the television series. Unfortunately, the reality is a long way removed from Hollywood. The fact is that Do is the hardest part of See, Feel, Think, Do. It has been estimated that CEOs consider implementation of strategy to be about six times harder than creating it. We think this is an underestimation.

According to Sahar Hashemi, co-founder of Coffee Republic, the UK high-street coffee chain:

> *The thing that separates entrepreneurs is really very simple. Whilst others dream, entrepreneurs see a good idea through to fruition. Whereas for most people an idea is cast aside after a couple of investigatory phone calls and perhaps a few discouraging comments from the so-called "experts," entrepreneurs don't quit, even when all they have to go on is gut instinct. They keep working hard to realize their dreams. The entrepreneurial mind thinks like this: "I don't have any experience, or special skills, I don't have the money. I have no idea how I'm going to do it. But I'm still going to do it."* [44]

One organization that has proved itself brilliant at execution is Tesco. It has moved from a distant fourth place in the UK market to becoming market leader and achieving a £2.5 billion profit for the financial year ending April 2006. Tim Mason, Tesco's president of US operations, puts this down to "Doing." He says, "We're quite good at strategic planning but what we're actually really good at is doing things – doing things for customers. We don't talk about it, we do it." We asked him why some organizations fail, and he said, "Most businesses have plans. Some business plans are better than ours. Where most businesses fall down is that they don't implement their plans." [45]

A case of how not to "Do" is Abbey, the UK based bank. In a blaze of publicity in September 2003 the bank launched a £11 million branding campaign intended to "turn banking on its head." The bank's 700 or so branches were rebranded and new advertising launched promising customers *"Abbey's straightforward attitude and simplified accounts will help you get on top of your money."* Unfortunately, the bank did not seem able to get on top of its own accounts. It reported losses of £686 million for the year ending 31 December 2003 in a year when most of its competitors reported record profits. It also failed to communicate the new strategy clearly to its employees or put in place the means to execute it. It lost the confidence of its people and as a result the brand experienced staff turnover 17 percent higher than the industry average.

Abbey was acquired by Banco Santander Central Hispano, the Spanish bank. The new head of sales and marketing, Graeme Hardie, said that not a single customer questioned by the bank has approved of the branding campaign carried out by the previous management and that the strategy had "confused customers and staff." Abbey's failure was one of execution. It had correctly identified that many consumers find financial matters confusing and would value a bank that made it easier for them to "keep on top of their money." Its error was in spending most of its budget on advertising this proposition before it had created the means to deliver it. What it failed to do was to put in place the nuts and bolts in the business that would ensure the new strategy's success.

EMC² AND THE "BIAS FOR ACTION"

In their book *Confronting Reality: Doing what matters to get things right*,[46] Larry Bossidy and Ram Charan make a compelling case for companies to focus on the basic building blocks of implementation to ensure a successful outcome. They tell the story of EMC² as a prime example of this.

In 2000 EMC², the high-tech information storage and management company, was the darling of Wall Street. Its revenues had risen from US$171 million in 1990 to US$8.9 billion by the end of 2000. Its stock price had increased faster in that 10-year period than any other listed stock in the New York Stock Exchange's history. The company was riding the crest of a wave as it entered 2001. In the first quarter of that year the wave crashed.

EMC² virtually owned the market for high-end information storage systems. Its Symmetrix system, priced in excess of US$500,000, was used by most large corporations around the world. Such was the demand that EMC² salespeople were known for their "take it or leave it" approach to pricing. If the customer couldn't or wouldn't pay, never mind, there were plenty of others wanting the product that would. As a result, EMC²'s gross margins were close to 60 percent, and it was achieving just over 20 percent at the bottom line. Nine percent of annual revenues were ploughed back into R&D so that the company could ensure it kept ahead of its competitors.

The culture of EMC² was, and is, one of a single-minded focus on execution and performance. Annual, quarterly, and monthly targets drive the business, and the highly disciplined sales force delivers against those targets. In short, EMC² was a highly tuned cash-generating machine, and the management team were appropriately confident about the future. Then the 2001 crash happened.

During the third quarter of 2001, the global environment continued to deteriorate, 9/11 happened, and sales fell off a cliff, taking profits and margins with them. Joe Tucci, the president and CEO, and his team were shocked by the numbers. Many of them had grown up with EMC² and had never seen anything like this before. Still, they were inclined to believe that this was a temporary correction before the market resumed its upward surge.

EMC²'s bullish sales people were in touch with their customers, but many of these were at the operational level, and the sales force was focused on the next month or quarter rather than the bigger picture. As a result, they too were convinced that it was simply a case of orders being delayed, and they continued to report any signs of business picking up again.

Joe Tucci was less convinced. He had joined what was then Wang Laboratories in the 1990s, when the company persisted with producing highly priced word processors after the PC had virtually made them obsolete. "We've got to assume at least a one-year downturn," Tucci told his team when he became EMC²'s president and CEO in January 2001. "And in these moments, great companies look in the mirror and become brutally honest. They commit to doing the hard things, as opposed to just trying to cut out costs and shuffle their way through the Street's expectations."

Tucci was not about to wait for the next quarter's results to confirm what his intuition was telling him: this was not a blip in the market. He didn't think about his action in terms of See, Feel, Think, Do, but that is exactly what he did. His first action was to go straight to see for himself what was happening. He met with CEOs and CFOs, the ultimate decision makers senior to the CIOs who were the customers for his products. What he learnt was sobering. They told him that there was a real economic slowdown which was hitting spending on high tech. In the face of falling revenues and with an excess of technology firms vying for business, customers were no longer prepared to pay a premium for top-end systems. Competitors like Hitachi and IBM were moving into EMC²'s territory with lower-priced machines that did most of what EMC²'s

Symmetrix system did. This was pay-back time for the aggressive EMC² salespeople.

Tucci realized that the business model that had served EMC² so well was no longer relevant to the new reality it was experiencing. He set out to dismantle the business model and create a new one that would enable the organization to thrive in the new world. The new strategy became clear: create new products that could compete effectively in the mid-market, reduce costs to offer better value, and ensure greater flexibility for customers. The only question was, could the company reorganize fast enough to implement the new strategy?

Over the next two years, storage prices fell by 40 percent each year. EMC²'s share of the high-end storage market fell from a high of 52 percent to 41 percent, and its gross margins fell to 32 percent from the previous high of roughly 60 percent. In 2002 EMC² declared a loss of US$119 million, a far cry from the giddy profit of US$1.8 billion it had posted as the new millennium began. This was indeed a new era, but was it one that would see the survival of EMC²? Tucci had his strategy. Now he had to "make it so."

Tucci and his team set about implementing their strategy, starting with annualized costs which were cut by US$1.3 billion to enable the firm to lower prices yet still support margins. Two levels were trimmed from management, and 30 percent of the workforce cut to create a leaner, faster-moving enterprise. The market was segmented into high, middle, and low-end sectors, and new products, platforms, and channels were created to service each. For example, the CLARiiON storage system designed for the mid-range market was to be distributed through Dell.

One thing Joe Tucci did not do was to slash investment in R&D. In fact he sustained R&D investment at 15 percent of revenues. He realized that this was needed more than ever. EMC² also acquired boutique software companies to enable it to provide complete information management solutions, a key requirement that he had heard from customers.

In order to implement all of these changes, EMC² needed new capabilities, processes, and people. The company was split into hardware and software divisions to increase the focus on these very different products. Cross-functional business management teams were formed, bringing together sales, product, and marketing people to align efforts at the very beginning of the development process. Tucci realized that new structures required new behaviors, and he couldn't afford to wait for them to develop. As a result he tripled the training budget to create a more customer-focused sales force, and give them the skills to sell solutions rather than merely write orders.

As the new EMC² gathered pace, so did the numbers. By the beginning of 2004 EMC² was growing at twice the rate of the market, and by the first quarter of 2005 it was reporting double-digit year-on-year revenue growth. First-quarter revenues grew to US$2.24 billion, 20 percent higher than the US$1.87 billion reported for the first quarter of 2004. Net income for the quarter 2005 was 93 percent higher than in the same quarter the previous year.

Announcing the first-quarter financial results, Tucci said this to analysts:

> EMC² delivered its seventh quarter in a row of double-digit revenue growth, once again extending one of the strongest and steadiest growth stories in the tech industry today. Solid execution and the investments we have made to broaden our product and market reach played major roles in our ability to successfully navigate through a difficult first quarter.

Joe Tucci and his team were certainly able to "Make it so" for EMC².

So how do we "Do"? Again, we have broken this concept down into three guiding principles which will hopefully help to turn vision into action:

- **Nuts and bolts.** What are the specific things we have to get right and put in place to make the perfect world a reality?

- **Magic dust.** How do we excite customers about what we are offering them and our people to deliver it?
- **Is it working?** How do we know we have succeeded?

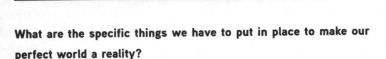

What are the specific things we have to put in place to make our perfect world a reality?

The EMC² story is a great demonstration of See, Feel, Think, and Do. Joe Tucci met with his customers as soon as he sensed there was a problem rather than wait for the next quarter's numbers to confirm it. He empathized with their concerns and then realized the implications for his business. He thought about what it would take to survive in the new reality, then got on and did it. The reason that the new strategy worked (and is producing record results as we go to press in mid-2005) is that he put in place the building blocks, the nuts and bolts necessary for success. New structures, training, product development processes, review mechanisms, and reporting systems all ensured that the strategy moved from rhetoric to reality.

Many organizations fail to execute change successfully because they lack the discipline to pay attention to the basic processes that create value in an organization. You cannot achieve different results without different behaviors, and you do not get different behaviors without different processes and practices. This requires careful attention to every component of the business model.

We have worked with many companies that have had grand plans for their brand or enhancing their customer experience. We have also seen some of these fail because executives put their faith in "change management." They thought that by bringing in consultants and organizing motivational events and the like, people would change their behavior and create different results. Well, sometimes they do – for a time. The problem is that the life of an event – no matter how good it is – can be measured in weeks rather than months. Without new leadership, skills, processes, structures, and reward mechanisms to back it up, the enthusiasm soon wanes, and people revert to old ways of working. Lord Marshall found this out the hard way when he was CEO of British Airways.

During the mid-1980s a major turnaround effort began at British Airways, which became known as the "PPF" or "Putting People First" program. Tasked with leading the airline into privatization by the Thatcher government, Colin Marshall (now Lord Marshall) quickly identified that the airline was operating on military lines rather than as a customer-focused business. Many of its senior managers were ex-Air Force pilots and engineers, and they tended to focus on the technical aspects of running an airline rather than the commercial aspects. Marshall realized that a complete reorientation was required to get everyone to understand that the airline existed for the benefit of passengers, not the other way round.

One of the ways this was achieved was the PPF program, which was a one-day communication event for several hundred employees at a time from across the business. For the first time ever, pilots would sit in the same room as check-in agents, baggage handlers, and cabin crew, to hear the same message at the same time. And that message was very clear: "We have to take better care of our customers, because if we don't, someone else will."

In the period that it took for all employees to go through this program, Colin Marshall attended almost every event, four days a week, every week for ten months. He spoke about his vision for the airline, but mainly he listened to employees in the open forum at the end of the day. What he heard was disturbing. The cabin crew, the very vanguard of the change, were hostile. What they told Marshall was, "You don't need to tell us to put customers first. Who do you think has been serving passengers when our management has been remote and preoccupied with jockeying for the best jobs?"

British Airways was, at this time, still trying to come to terms with the merger of BOAC and BEA some years earlier. The cabin crew went on to tell Marshall, "Give us management that takes an interest in our work and will support us with processes and equipment that work, and we will take care of the customers."

Marshall listened carefully, and PPF was quickly followed by "Managing People First" (MPF), designed to ensure that every manager was aware of how he or she fitted into the airline, and how his or her role impacted colleagues and subordinates. As a result of MPF every department was tasked with overhauling its processes, roles, and systems to ensure they were aligned with the vision for the company.

This experience at BA and practical experience in working with a number of international companies led to the development of the Organizational Alignment Survey®[47] (OAS) in the early 1990s. The OAS® model comprises 12 key factors. Research found that these 12 factors are statistically related to an organization's ability to achieve tangible business results.

The 12 factors are as follows:

- **Market focus:** the extent to which management are engaged with customers and have an accurate view of the marketplace. EMC^2 was almost caught out by the change in the external market, and only swift action to engage with customers improved the focus.

- **Vision, mission, and strategy:** the clarity of direction, and the extent to which this is aligned with target customer needs. How connected are the company vision, mission, and strategy, and how consistent are they with one another? (In some organizations these are produced by different executives at different times to achieve different ends, and they are rarely aligned.) EMC^2's strategy of offering high-end proprietary systems was out of step with the emerging need. The vision, mission, and strategy were therefore changed to re-task the organization.

- **Culture:** the "DNA" of the organization and the way things gets done. Culture comprises the values and principles that drive behavior, and the extent to which they support the strategy. For example, the aggressive sales-led culture in EMC^2 needed to change to one of listening to customers and working cross-functionally.

- **People policies:** HR systems that reinforce or support the strategy. The response in EMC^2 was to triple the training budget and align reward systems with the desired behavior.

- **Climate:** the level of morale in the organization and quality of internal communications to support the change. Joe Tucci said, "Communication is all about synchronization and harmony – understanding the benefits to the customer, and synchronizing processes, vision, mission, and culture."

- **Standards and procedures:** these form the operating system that translates good intentions into reality. The way that the work gets done and the processes necessary to support it have to change if the strategy is to be realized. The introduction of business management teams was one way that EMC^2 changed the way it brought products to market.

- **Service:** this is about the way the product is delivered through the customer-focused behavior of people. Key account managers in EMC^2 were tasked with focusing on the needs of important customers and bringing the capabilities of the organization to bear on achieving solutions.

- **Quality:** the relative quality of the product or service compared with competitive products. EMC^2 had always had a fine reputation for the quality of its products, but it began to lose the edge in terms of their flexibility in interfacing with customer systems. The introduction of new software rectified this.

- **Differentiation:** the extent to which the organization is seen as different and valuable by customers. EMC^2 has increasingly focused on information management rather than simply storage as a way of differentiating from other hardware manufacturers. Sophisticated systems allow the customer to retrieve information on an as-needed basis.

- **Performance tracking:** the extent to which the organization measures its performance on the things that matter to customers rather than the things that are easy to measure. EMC^2 measures financial performance very rigorously, but also tracks how its customers rate their experience with the organization.

- **Sustaining performance:** the ability of the company to reinvent itself when required. The reason that EMC^2 is thriving today, unlike some of the high-tech companies who suffered in the dot.bomb crash, is that Joe Tucci and his team were able to realign all aspects of their business model to maintain competitive edge and thus sustain their financial performance.

- **Leadership:** this lies at the heart of the model. Without effective leadership none of the other factors can happen effectively, and even if by accident they do, they certainly will not be aligned with the other components. Effective leaders are articulate and intentional about managing each of these 12 dimensions, so that they "walk the talk" rather than "stumble the mumble" when the time comes to execute their strategy. Leadership also encompasses the See, Feel, Think, and Do skills we have already discussed.

In 2001 the OAS® survey was subjected to a very thorough update, following which it was independently validated by Dr David Matsumoto of San Francisco State University. Responses were correlated from over 23,000 OAS® respondents from 52 companies, representing a variety of industries, and across 20 countries. The 60 statements of the survey were then correlated against six business results areas. The 10 statements with which employees in the high-performing organizations most agreed, and which correlated most highly with the overall improved business results achieved by these companies, were:

1 We are a highly successful organization.

2 We have a well-defined strategy to overcome competitors.

3 We match the claims made through our advertising and promotion.

4 Employees are well trained to meet the performance standards required by their jobs.

5 We measure our quality/service performance against the world's best organizations in our field.

6 Managers meet with customers and consumer groups on a regular basis.

7 We carefully monitor the product/service quality of our suppliers, distributors, and agents.

8 Employees are regularly briefed on departmental and organizational performance.

9 There is good cooperation among all departments in my organization.

10 Performance targets that my department sets are realistic and consistent with our organizational vision/mission.[48]

The 12 dimensions of the OAS® are the "nuts and bolts" of the organization, which have to be tightened, tuned, and tested to ensure that the organization moves from "Think" to "Do." But sometimes we need a little bit of magic too.

MAGIC DUST

How do we get our customers excited about our offer and our people excited about delivering it?

The advertising agency Grey Worldwide commissioned a survey called "Eye on Australia" to capture the view of Australian consumers on business. One of its findings was that 59 percent of the consumers surveyed disagreed when asked whether marketing and advertising helped people to shop better. Not surprisingly, only 15 percent of marketers disagreed. We suspect that a similar result would be obtained in many markets.

While we know that advertising does influence consumers, even if it is at the subliminal level, the fact is that most consumers are becoming increasingly jaded with advertising and promotion. It has been estimated that the average consumer is exposed to in the region of 3,000 marketing messages a day. As humans, we are programmed to screen out data that is not necessary to our survival, and so much of this simply becomes background noise. It takes something special to raise a product or service to the level that we become conscious of it. *The measure "share of voice" is almost dead. The real metric is "share of mind."*

If we were to ask you to go online to buy books, the chances are that you will type the words Amazon.com into your browser. Why? Is it because Amazon conducts expensive television campaigns or extensive print advertising? No, it is more likely that previous positive experiences of Amazon have made this brand top of mind when it comes to buying books online. It has a share of your mind. In fact Amazon.com grew from start-up to US$3 billion in sales in just six years, largely without advertising as we know it. Sure, it had extensive links on the web, but most of its growth was through viral marketing: customers experiencing the brand and then recommending it to others. Amazon has one of the highest "advocacy" ratios in the market. A very high proportion of its customers are happy to recommend the brand.

Creating share of mind needs more than just good marketing or even good service: it needs a little bit of magic, because it requires the customer to engage with the brand in a way that endows the product with "an indelible memory," to quote Tom Ford, former chief designer at Gucci.

BANYAN TREE: RESORTING TO ROMANCE

The Banyan Tree is a luxury chain of hotels and resorts which has been voted Asia's best resort experience and one of the world's best places to stay by *Condé Nast Traveller* magazine. The brand is targeted at couples, and it promises "sanctuary for the senses." The Banyan Tree has a tremendously loyal following from its customers because of the magic it performs every day. The magic comes not from doing anything mysterious, but in the overall effect that the service has on customers. Disney World has the same impact. It is the combination of all of the "nuts and bolts" being assembled in a way that leaves an indelible memory on the guest.

The "sanctuary for the senses" proposition permeates everything the brand does, even the prosaic turn-down service. The Banyan Tree uses a Thai concept called *gan eng*, which literally means "lightening of the mood." This is best illustrated by the "intimate moments" service which is available to guests if they wish. The aim is to transform the customary bed turn-down into something magical and memorable. While you are away at dinner, staff decorate your villa with 50 candles, and make up the sleeping area with silk sheets sprinkled with orchid petals. Special burners fill the room with the smell of Banyan Tree's own brand of aromatic essence, and the villa resounds to the soothing sounds of a special Banyan Tree CD. The outdoor bath is filled with warm water, and relaxing oils added to it, once again the resort's own brand made from traditional Thai ingredients. Finally, if you wish, the Banyan Tree's in-house trained therapists will be on hand to provide a massage to you and your partner. The brand has taken the mundane turn-down service which every luxury hotel offers, and turned it into something which is "on-brand" and truly a magical experience.

Mr Kamal Chaoui, former area general manager of the Banyan Tree, related how "the concept was designed around the sensory pleasures of our guests. The guest experience was designed to recreate the cultural rituals from the Thai village and simulate the sense of sight, touch and smell involved in a traditional village spa." The Banyan Tree stimulates the "See and Feel" dimensions. The "Think and Do" part are best left to the guests!

But *gan eng* is not just about lightening the mood of customers. The Banyan Tree employees are a vital factor, and the management pays a great deal of attention to them, even to the extent of building a childcare center and school for employees' children. Kamal Chaoui explained:

> The notion of success and achievement here is very different to the Western model. Many of our people come from the local communities, and for them it is very important to feel part of what the Banyan Tree stands for. The success of the business comes from the success of the community.

The Banyan Tree creates a guest experience that goes way beyond good service, and delivers its brand promise in a way that is so unique as to make customers its best salespeople. The employees are an integral part of this process. It is a totally holistic way of thinking about the brand. That is the very essence of "Do": combining magic and execution to create something a little bit special. But how do you go about achieving this in a large organization?

CATHAY PACIFIC: DESTINATION EXCELLENCE

Cathay Pacific Airways has long had a reputation for providing exceptional in-flight service. However, that same reputation did not extend to its ground service in the mid-1990s. In fact customer satisfaction levels were tracking at about 50 percent of the level for in-flight service. Derek Smith, the general manager for Cathay's Ground Service division at that time, was determined to do something about it. We had the good fortune to work with Derek and his team on what became known as "Destination Excellence." The program was soon given its own three-letter destination code, DEX.

Our research showed that a large part of the problem was low self-esteem on the part of the ground staff, and a lack of alignment with the in-flight service department and the needs of the passengers. The staff felt that they were second-class citizens in the shadow of the more glamorous flight attendants. They were unclear as to the importance of their role and the impact they had on Cathay Pacific passengers. We agreed that some behavioral training was going to be important, but first we had to change attitudes and get them to engage more with the Cathay Pacific brand. We needed to bring a little bit of magic to check-in.

Envelopes soon started to arrive at the homes of the several thousand ground staff, inviting them to a one day event to be held at the Sheraton Hotel, Kowloon. Enclosed within the envelope was a Cathay Pacific First Class ticket to "Destination Excellence."

When the employees arrived at the Sheraton they were directed to a large foyer that had been transformed into a check-in area. Manning the desks were their own managers, who greeted them warmly and issued boarding cards with their seat number for the "flight." The staff then "boarded" and were greeted at the door of the ballroom by First Class flight attendants, who greeted and seated the awestruck delegates. The morning began with a welcome aboard announcement, and continued with video interviews with passengers, talking about their experiences. Through a series of high-energy presentations and interactive exercises, the employees came to understand more about how they fitted into the airline, and the importance of their role in creating positive impressions.

At lunchtime the "flight touched down in Hawaii for a refueling stop." As the delegates left the ballroom they found that the foyer had been transformed into a tropical destination complete with steel bands, palm trees, and barbecues. Following lunch they reboarded for the flight back to Hong Kong, and were introduced to the notion of "We have magic to do." This was a simple process of helping all the delegates understand that through their behavior and speech they could add tremendous value to the passengers' experience.

A sophisticated businessperson reading this from today's perspective might think it superficial, or even a bit corny, but for these very junior ground staff, many of whom had never flown before or even been a customer of a major Western hotel, the day was a truly magical (and memorable) experience.

As we said earlier, events alone are insufficient, and the DEX events were quickly followed by skills training, new performance measurement schemes, reward systems, and communications. In the year following DEX customer satisfaction levels for ground handling rose to the same level as for in-flight service, and they stayed that way. In order to sustain a high-performing organization, measurement is vital.

IS IT WORKING?

How do we know if we are succeeding?

The driver of the DEX program was the need to improve customer satisfaction scores. We introduced this book by saying that we feel that the pendulum has swung too far towards scientific management, IQ, and hard data. We have argued that experience management, EQ, and intuition are just as important, if not more so. But this does not mean that we do not subscribe to the importance of measurement. The fact is that without a clear goal and a way of measuring our progress towards it, we can just as easily swing too far the other way.

The challenge is to find ways of managing the "soft stuff," not just the "hard stuff." Most organizations base their measurement on what is easy to measure (usually quantitative), rather than what is important to customers (often qualitative).

One industry where measurement is vital is the clinical trials business. Pharmaceutical companies compete against one another to bring new drugs to market, and doing so more quickly than competing firms can make a difference of US$500 million in potential revenues for a major drug like Viagra.

Clinical trials are the means by which major pharmaceutical companies test medicines to ensure that they are ready to bring to market. The trialing process is very complex and difficult because it requires the drug companies to develop test kits, distribute these to sites like hospitals and clinics, then arrange for the completed tests to be shipped back to their laboratories for analysis. Usually transporting these completed tests requires the use of hazardous material like dry ice. A typical large-scale trial requires 10,000 individual test sites all requiring kits, distribution, and transportation of the completed test in controlled conditions. No wonder then that "Reducing time to market can make a difference of US$1.3 million per day," according to Onno Boots, director of global account management at TNT, one of the world's largest transportation and logistics companies.

TNT AND INCREASING SPEED TO MARKET

TNT's Global Account division exists to identify and grow new segments of the market. TNT, like many other transportation companies, had been involved in supporting the clinical trials market for many years. But it was only when Onno and his team went out to speak with the pharma companies, doctors, and clinical research companies involved in the process that they realized just how fragmented and inefficient the process was. They spent time with each of the key stakeholders, and looked at the logistics providers at that time. What they quickly realized was that if TNT could provide a full end-to-end experience for the clinical trials market, it would have tremendous benefits for all the stakeholders. But could it make money?

As they developed their thinking further it became apparent that the overall market was worth about US$0.5 billion, and that because of the huge benefits in being able to reduce the time to market, it would be a high-margin business for any company that could organize itself to deliver across the whole value chain. The numbers were so big that TNT appointed an external consultant to verify its figures and validate its conclusions. The answer came back: yes, the market was there, and yes, it could be very profitable. But could TNT do it?

One of the things that the team learnt was that TNT was not a credible player in the clinical trials market. It was not associated with the medical profession, and had not carved out a reputation for handling these kinds of materials. Finally, the nature of the business is one where a great deal of expertise is required to achieve the level of confidence in the results that the drug administrations demand. It became clear that executing against this business opportunity would require a great deal of attention to the nuts and bolts as well as a fair sprinkling of magic.

This is where Chris Goossens, director of customer experience for TNT, enters the picture. Chris and her team mapped the entire clinical trials process, and analyzed the skills, knowledge, and competencies required. They looked at their own internal structure, and reorganized into one dedicated team, to exist within TNT but branded as the Clinical Trials Network (CTN). All of the staff in the new operation were sent out to attend every conference and seminar they could to acquire the industry-specific knowledge needed, but also to rub shoulders with the clinicians, doctors, and scientists they would be dealing with, and to learn their language, concerns, and suggestions. This led to creating a new end-to-end experience and the plan to implement it. According to Onno Boots, this central master plan which specified all of the goals, activities, and performance measures required to operationalize the new business was the single biggest factor that led to success.

CTN today stretches from Europe to Asia and the United States, with major hubs located in each continent. Every partner in the process is seamlessly linked to every other via a web-based tracking system which is 50 percent faster than previous methods, and completely transparent, so that stakeholders can track trials as they occur. The business has seen double-digit growth over the past three years, with 33 percent growth in the last year alone. The CTN story illustrates the power of seeing a market need, empathizing with the stakeholders to understand their concerns, thinking about what it would take to turn this into a successful business, and then executing this impeccably.

All of the companies we have featured so far have had success because they not only thought differently, they dared to do differently. And at the heart of all their thinking and their continual quest to improve what they do is a simple and powerful question – in fact, it is such an important question to See, Feel, Think, Do that it deserves a separate chapter. Unless as an organization you are prepared to ask this simple question repeatedly, you will never be able to make the transformations in customer experience or the leaps in business that will bring the greatest success. That simple question is: "Why?"

THE POWER
OF "WHY?"

Anyone who has spent any time at all with small children hates this one question more than any other. "Why?" It is so irritating because it is so deceptively simple. "Why is the sky blue, mum?" "Why do I have to go to bed early?" "Why do we have to go to the shops?" "Why are we going to see Aunty Joan if you don't like her?" "Why can't we go by car?" "Why can't I have this toy?" It's the particularly insistent tone of the repeated "Why?" that gets under the skin; that, and the fact that the ultimate answer you have as an adult to a child's repetition of "Why?" is "Because it just is!" Although this brings closure to the debate, it is somehow intellectually unsatisfying.

Maybe it's because we are ultimately discouraged as children from asking "Why?" by the grumpy finality of our elders' and betters' responses that, as we get older, we fall out of the habit of asking this most inconvenient question. Whatever the case, the truth is that we take so much of our life on trust, we accept the way things are, and rarely ask why things are the way they are. Even less often do we ask, "Why can't things be different?"

Yet as we said in Think, it is precisely our ability to question our circumstances, to try to understand who we are, where we have come from, what we are doing, and where we are going, and through asking to change our lives for the better, that distinguishes us as human beings from all other life on this planet. We should encourage ourselves and others to ask "Why?" more often: to encourage an inquiring mind, a restless curiosity to challenge what is presented to us, not in order to reject it but so that we can understand it, so we can learn from it and perhaps even improve it.

It's true in general of life. Why am I in this job? Why am I voting for this political party? Why do I want to live in this house? Why do I want to marry this person? Why is this person my friend? All these are questions that are worth asking ourselves more than once.

And it is true in the field of human invention, and in the development of the many things that have enhanced our lives. Let's take one invention that has transformed the quality of life and life expectancy for hundreds of millions of people: the humble vaccination. Two hundred and fifty years ago, smallpox was endemic to Britain, and the cause of death or at least disfiguration for hundreds of thousands of people. Anyone could be susceptible to it, and it made no distinction on the basis of age, sex, or class of birth. But one country doctor, Edward Jenner, observed a particular phenomenon by talking to one of his patients. A milkmaid told him that she could not get smallpox because she had already had cowpox. Jenner was skeptical, but he noticed that milkmaids tended to be spared the disease even when others in their family had caught it. He wondered why. So he asked more questions and discovered that all these maids who had been unaffected by smallpox in their families had been infected by the far less serious cowpox – a virus picked up from cows.

Jenner began to explore the link more closely, and realized that when exposed to small doses of a virus similar to the smallpox virus, the body built up a resistance and immunity to smallpox. So he did something about it: he took a small amount of the cowpox virus and gave it to people who had not yet had smallpox. Vaccination was born (from the Latin word *vacca*, which means cow), and smallpox and subsequently many other diseases were history.

Wherever we look in the world of human achievement, it is the power of observation unlocked by the restless questioning "Why?" that has been at the root of success. We can fly to the moon because a succession of people, from Da Vinci to the Wright brothers, to Chuck Yeager to John F. Kennedy, asked, "Why can't we?" The United States has nearly universal car ownership because Henry Ford asked, "Why can't every American have a car?" In the early 1970s, Thomas Watson Sr., President of IBM, estimated that there was a worldwide market for about three computers. In the same decade, Steve Jobs asked the question, "Why can't there be a computer in every home?" We have built bridges across vast stretches of water, built a tunnel to unite the United Kingdom with continental Europe, climbed the highest mountains, grown crops in the desert, and cloned human cells. And somewhere along the line someone asked, "Why?" And someone asked, "Why not?"

But in business we do not often enough ask "Why?" and "Why not?" Nor do we know how to ask "Why?" That is not the case with all the companies and businesses we have featured in this book. One of the most important characteristics they have in common is that they constantly ask "Why?" They are endlessly curious about their customers, constantly thoughtful about their products, services, or marketing, and continuously looking to understand and improve the experience they provide. And they encourage the people who work for them also to ask "Why?"

Do you remember the film *Big*, with Tom Hanks? He plays a 10-year-old kid who is suddenly transformed into a man after making a wish, and ends up getting a job in a toy company. There are two famous scenes. In one Hanks dances on a floor piano with the CEO, helping the CEO to get back in touch with the sheer joy of toys, which is what his consumers need to feel, of course.

The other famous scene is set in the boardroom. One of the top executives (the film's bad guy) is making a slick marketing presentation about competitors, retail trends, profitability, and so on, all of which is designed to recommend the case for a new toy. The new toy is in the boardroom, as is the Tom Hanks character, and it is being passed around all the executives, all of whom have applauded the speech and are endorsing the product. All of them – except Tom Hanks. He has not been concentrating on the speech, he has been examining the toy, and he reckons it will never sell. The most important moment follows, because the CEO leans forward and simply asks Tom Hanks to explain why he thinks it won't sell. Of course, Tom Hanks tells the board in simple, child-like language exactly why it is nowhere near as good as the competitors' toys, but what they could do to make it better. The CEO hears his reasons, pauses, then decides to discontinue the product.

Two things happened in this scene. First, the CEO asked "Why?" and second, Tom Hanks expressed himself in the simple, direct language of the consumer, not the jargon of the marketing man. He challenged the way things were with the simple-mindedness and sense of wonder of a child. And Amazon and "one click," Apple and the iPod, Sony and the Walkman, Heinz and its kids' ketchups, the Geek Squad, Progressive, Innocent, The Carphone Warehouse, Vodafone: they have all asked why are things the way they are and why they can't be better, in a simple, direct way that is almost "child-like," to quote Charles Dunstone.

THE ART OF ASKING "WHY?"

There are many ways to ask "Why?" and many areas of the customer or brand experience to interrogate. The trick to asking "Why?" is simply to be specific and to dare to ask the simplest question. Like the little boy who asked "Why is the Emperor wearing no clothes, mummy?" it is often the simplest and most specific question, which no one else has dared or bothered to ask, that can have the most profound effect. Amazon did not ask, "Why aren't people buying more online?" Instead it asked, "Why can't people get their shopping done at the click of a button?"

Also phrasing a question "Why ...?" forces you to be more detailed, more forensic, and more focused in your answer. It pushes you to think in a structured way about all the reasons that could be affecting any one thing. Asking "Why?" can lead to great changes. In this chapter we have assembled a selection of stories that show how people in business have asked "Why?" and what they have done in response. Always it is a very personal issue that has made them ask "Why?" Perhaps because it is only when we really care about something that we can bother to ask, "Why is it like that?" and "Why can't it be different?"

Why is this queue so long? Tesco and the "line of one."

A question kept bothering Tesco. Why do customers always have to queue at the checkout when there are two or three unused counters? Why can't we just open them too? The answer was simple: nobody had bothered to ask the question before. Lines of responsibility in a supermarket were strictly demarcated. If you were a shelf stacker, you stacked shelves; if you were a checkout operative, you worked on a checkout. If there were not enough checkout operatives to staff all the checkouts, then checkouts remained closed, even if the shelf stackers had spare time.

"Why can't we change this?" asked Tesco. There was no reason other than that was the way things had always been done. So Tesco introduced its "line of one" concept. In-store staff were now trained to do a multiplicity of tasks, so that every part of the customer experience was everyone's responsibility. For example, a shelf stacker could staff a checkout till if needed. The concept was simply this: if there is a line with more than one customer in it, we should open another till until all the tills are staffed. It made one of the most tedious and stressful parts of the shopping experience so much easier. And it was proof of their brand promise that "Every little helps."

Why do people have to wait till they die before they get their life insurance payout? Prudential Canada and the living needs benefit.

Ron Barbaro of Prudential Canada, one of the country's leading insurance providers, was driving home after visiting a terminally ill friend. He was saddened by his friend's plight, but also troubled by one of the paradoxes of his profession in life insurance: the money that you have saved all your life only comes to you when you are dead. "His life insurance is useless at the moment," thought Ron about his friend, "since it's not unlocked until he dies." So Ron asked himself a profound "Why?" question: "Why can't you get the money you need when you are dying rather than when you are dead?"

How can you die before you die? This impossible question led to Prudential introducing a new insurance product called a living needs product. It was a unique product that paid out before death. Now every major life company offers a living needs benefit-type policy.

ASKING "WHY?" CAN LEAD TO A MULTI-MILLION DOLLAR BUSINESS

Why does my vacuum cleaner always get blocked? James Dyson and the bagless cleaner.

In 1978, James Dyson was puzzled and infuriated by an everyday household occurrence: his vacuum cleaner was constantly losing its power to suck up dirt. Asking "Why?" he opened up his machine and saw that dust quickly clogged the pores of the bag inside it, which meant that its airflow was obstructed and hence the suction power dropped rapidly.

He then asked himself another "Why?": "Why do I need a bag?" If you could get rid of the bag you would get rid of the obstruction, and also you would get rid of the annoying and dusty process of changing the bag. It took him five years and 5,127 prototypes, but eventually he designed the world's first cyclonic bagless vacuum cleaner. But his quest for answers to difficult questions didn't stop there. Great invention though it undoubtedly was, no company seemed to want it. Why would they reject a bagless cleaner? The answer was probably that at the time the market for selling vacuum cleaner bags was worth US$500 million. As Mike Rutter, Hoover's vice president for Europe, would later say on national television in the United Kingdom, with his tongue in cheek, "I regret that Hoover as a company did not take the product technology off Dyson; it would have lain on the shelf and not been used."

So James Dyson then asked, "Why not make it on my own?" And since he asked that question, he and his research team have developed products that have achieved sales of over US$10 billion.

ASKING "WHY?" CAN SAVE MONEY AND IMPROVE CUSTOMERS' EXPERIENCE

Why are we serving long lunches on short-haul flights? Midwest Express and the on-board baked cookies.

Midwest Express has been one of the most successful and innovative short-haul airlines in the United States. Its slogan, "The best care in the air," has driven its approach to customer service, and it encourages and empowers its employees to generate ideas that can improve the customer's experience. One example of this is the story of its on-board cookies. An in-flight attendant thought it was ridiculous that on a one or two-hour flight, the airline would serve large meals at the seat. By the time the plane had taken off, the seat belt signs had come off and the food was served, it was time to take the food tray away again. So the attendant asked, "Why do we bother? Why don't we just give them a cake and a coffee? That's all they really want."

From that question came the idea of baking fresh cookies on board the plane. It not only gave people the appropriate snack, but the smell of the freshly baked cookies made for a very pleasant ambience. And as we found in our book *Uncommon Practice* it saved the company around US$80,000 a year by not having to spend so much on catering.

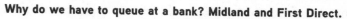
Why do we have to queue at a bank? Midland and First Direct.

In the 1980s the Midland Bank liked to advertise itself as the "Listening bank." Well, what it heard from its customers was not great! People simply disliked having to wait in long queues at the branches for often poor, slow, or unhelpful service. However, the story goes that there was a "pocket" of customers who expressed satisfaction with the bank. Why were these the only people satisfied? They all had one thing in common as customers: they never went to a bank branch!

That insight must have helped Midland as it pressed ahead with an innovation that would transform banking in the United Kingdom: telephone or direct banking. Already trialed successfully in the United States, Midland brought the concept over to the United Kingdom, branded it First Direct, and promised a bank that would go at exactly the pace that its customers wanted to go. It even ran two advertising campaigns on different television channels at the same time, and offered people the choice of which advert they would prefer to watch. First Direct has been much imitated, but nothing has exceeded the tremendous customer loyalty it engenders. Every five seconds, a First Direct customer recommends the bank to someone else – and there is no queue to join!

Why can't we keep acting like a small business even when we have grown? Lush Cosmetics and its culture.

In 1994 Mark Constantine opened his first Lush Cosmetics store in the King's Road, Chelsea. Mark had for years made environmentally friendly cosmetics and beauty products, first for The Body Shop and later for his own branded company Cosmetics To Go, which went bankrupt. Mark knew that there was a market for his products: ones that were exotic, pampering, made from natural ingredients which respected the environment and reflected the differing cultures from which the ingredients came. Within 10 years Lush comprised 192 stores worldwide, 40 in the United Kingdom, and 2,000 employees. By 2003 it had reached sales of £50 million for the 12 months to June and recorded a post-tax profit of £1.5 million.

But one question has continually bugged Mark and his team: why does getting bigger often seem to mean that companies lose the "specialness" which made them so distinctive when they were smaller or just starting out? Mark's answer to this question is that they don't need to if they stick to the first principles, and instead of creating one bigger business, create what feels more like a group of smaller companies. So as Lush has grown it has refused to compromise. All products remain hand made, all ingredients remain the freshest and often the most expensive that can be found (including a jasmine which is more valuable than gold!), and there are no artificial additives or preservatives used. Instead of creating factories to mass produce its products, Lush has simply hired more people to make more products by hand. And it has a simple mantra: it only works with people it likes.

Why would people buy our drink if we can't afford a big advertising budget? Red Bull and guerrilla marketing.

Dietrich Mateschitz was sitting in the bar of the Mandarin Oriental in Hong Kong when he was served a vodka with Red Bull, a Thai tonic drink which an entrepreneur Chaleo Yoovidhya had been marketing as a "pick me up" and healthy energizer in Asia. Dietrich was impressed by the drink and its use as a mixer. He observed immediately its potential as a trendy drink for young Europeans. In 1987 he began selling Red Bull in Austria, his home market, and within 12 years, worldwide sales had reached US$1 billion.

Why? There were two reasons. First was, of course, his own insight and intuition when sitting in that Hong Kong hotel, which made him realize the possible audience for the drink. The second was the highly unusual (at the time) approach to marketing the product internationally – one of the most successful examples of what is now known as "guerrilla marketing." The soft drinks market was dominated for years by major players that had mass distribution and deep pockets for advertising spend. The basic formula was to launch a hugely expensive media campaign to raise awareness and encourage trial of a new soft drink, and to flood the distribution channels (on and off premises, supermarkets, confectioners, newsagents, and tobacconists) with the product. In the absence of such distribution power and the spend to build the relevant image, why would anyone want to sell a drink that was odd tasting, with an odd name and an odd proposition?

Dietrich already had the answer, of course. It was the one he had when he was first served the vodka–Red Bull mixer in the Mandarin Oriental: because it was "cool." And if it was "cool" it would have to be marketed in a "cool" way: it had to "catch on" as a craze by being carefully targeted and distributed in the first instance. Dietrich and his teams therefore adopted the following marketing strategies for the brand. First they would take a different approach to distribution. Instead of trying to "piggy back" off a major distributor, offering to cover the distributor's costs of sales promotions and give trade discounts in return for a chance to get some shelf space, they would either target small distributors and gain an exclusive distribution agreement, or hire their own warehouse to keep volumes of the product and then employ teams of young people (representative of the target market) to go around and sell the product in local stores, bars, and clubs. Second, they had a clear idea of whom their target market was and how to reach them without advertising. They targeted 16–29 year olds who aspired to a "cool" lifestyle that centered on activities that required high levels of energy and adrenaline, such as clubbing. Red Bull would hunt out the clubs and bars where their target customers would hang out. Then, to encourage trial of the brand, they would hire people to hand out samples of the drink or encourage bar staff to recommend it to their customers, as a way of "keeping the night going."

As well as targeting these clubs and bars, they also associated themselves with alternative sports, as these had particular cachet with the target group. So in the United Kingdom, for example, they would pitch up stalls and posters at skateboard parks, handing out drinks and linking the energy proposition with the desire to have a fun, adrenaline-filled life. "Red Bull gives you wings" was the slogan that the company adopted. In the United States the company sponsored the Red Bull Huckfest, a ski and snowboard freestyle event which was exactly the kind of event its target audience would recognize both as cool and as requiring extreme energy. This "guerrilla" activity rapidly established the brand's credentials as the "authentic" drink for clubbing, sports, and for any kind of pick-me-up (including morning hangovers after a heavy night on the vodka–Red Bulls!). Only when the brand has been properly introduced and established in a market does the business invest in traditional media, and that is only to reinforce the brand's personality and proposition.

The Red Bull brand has been one of the most celebrated successes of the last decade; it virtually single-handedly grew the energy drinks market worldwide, and it is now estimated that over 1 billion cans of the drink have been sold around the world.

Its success was down to someone seeing, feeling, thinking, and then doing something very different. Faced with a small business and a big idea, Mateschitz asked, "Why do we have to behave like any other soft drink? Why can't we build a billion-dollar brand without using a big advertising campaign?" And his success has shown the answers to those questions.

THE RULES OF ASKING "WHY?"

"Why" is, then, the most important question you can ask in marketing, in business – possibly even in life itself. But remember the rules of asking why:

- Ask a very specific "Why?" Focus on either a part of the customer experience, or a customer behavior, or a particular feature or trend in any marketplace (remember Tesco and the checkout counters).
- Phrase your question in the simplest language, language that your customers will be likely to understand. The simpler and more direct the question, the less ambiguous the answer is likely to be (remember Midland Bank and First Direct).
- Be prepared to ask the "awkward" question, even if you think it might seem like a stupid one. It is often only by challenging the fundamental preconceptions that everyone shares that any significant change can be made (remember Ron Barbaro and his "How can you die before you die?" question).

All the companies that we have featured in this book have dared to ask "Why?" and they have dared to ask "Why not?" At the root of their success, we believe, is a restless curiosity, the endless desire for insight and information that can help them improve the experience of their customers, the working lives of their employees, and the fortunes of their businesses. It might not be rocket science, but the right way to ask "why" is still uncommon practice.

ANDY SMITH
SPECIAL

Geek
Squad

AGENT

903

SUMMARY: PUTTING IT TOGETHER

We have shared stories from many of the companies that we think best illustrate See, Feel, Think, Do principles. As we have related the stories, we have attempted to illustrate why we feel that while simple in concept, See, Feel, Think, Do is harder to implement in practice. It's one of those common sense/uncommon practice things that we like so much. But the real power comes in bringing these four elements together, so in this last chapter we shall tell some stories of organizations that use all of the principles. You can be the judge of the extent to which these stories illustrate See, Feel, Think, Do, and the three elements that underpin each.

THE GEEK SQUAD

SEE

It was while Robert Stephens was studying computer science at the University of Minnesota in the early 1990s that he landed a job fixing computers for the Human Factors Research Laboratory. He began to notice the mergers and consolidations taking place between computer companies; he saw that the products were getting more powerful and more complex with e-mail, Internet connections and new software all conspiring to make it more difficult for average users to configure themselves. He observed that there was little technical support for these customers, and what support was available was often inconsistent, unreliable with generally poor levels of service. Robert saw an opportunity: to create a firm that would provide technical support and be differentiated through the service it offered.

Stephens went out to speak with customers, suppliers and computer firms to really find out what it would take to create a different kind of company. He learnt that most computer support firms were staffed by techies with little understanding of customers or service, so he took his inspiration from hotels and restaurants. How did the best treat their customers? How did they differentiate? How did the customers feel as a result?

FEEL

When a computer crashes the customer is anxious, angry but most of all, concerned to get it back up again quickly. Stephens soon realized that the keys to success were rapid response and adaptability. Customers did not expect technical support firms to be either of these, and so by building a business around these factors he could be successful. He also realized that customers took it for granted that their computer was going to be fixed eventually, but it was the overall experience that left them fuming, so he needed to create a new kind of experience to win in the market. The big idea came when he was waiting for a computer to boot up one day. What could he do to fill that awkward time and reduce the level of customer anxiety? And in a soft-focus kind of moment the answer came: why not get the customer laughing? And so the idea of the Geek Squad was born, and their motto, "We'll save your ass."

THINK

The idea came in part from films like *Ghostbusters* and the 1960s television show *Dragnet*. Why not have a mobile squad of support people who could fix customers' technical problems quickly but with style and humour? Stephens didn't do any research other than observing and listening to customers, but he just knew that the idea would be successful. So in April 1994 the Geek Squad was born with US$200.

Four or five months after starting Stephens hired his first

employee – closely followed by his first "Special Agent." When a customer calls they will get a rapid and totally reliable response by a Special Agent who arrives driving a "Geekmobile" emblazoned with the Geek Squad insignia. The Special Agent will be wearing a uniform straight out of Mission Control and NASA in the 1960s: white short-sleeve shirt, black clip-on tie, black trousers with white socks and, of course, heavy black-framed spectacles. How else would a geek dress? But Stephens is quick to point out that the uniform is not a gimmick.

Our uniforms serve a purpose, they are machine washable so agents can keep them clean, they are made from breathable fabric so that the guys don't get sweaty and most of all, they keep us humble and remind us that we are less important than the customer. You cannot wear our uniform and have an ego.

Of course the uniforms also add a note of humor, which is carried through when the agent flips open his badge "Dragnet" style and in a Humphrey Bogart drawl announces, "Good morning ma'am, I'm from the Geek Squad."

DO

Stephens was starting on a shoestring but was determined not to bring in investors who would try to dilute his concept. So he started slow and found innovative ways to save costs, buying up old vintage cars for example because of their unique look from other cars on the road. He didn't need to market because "If you provide great service your competitors become your biggest source of business because they are so bad." Advertising? Easy, just make it company policy that Special Agents must drive their cars exactly two miles slower than the speed limit. That way most cars will pass them and see the Geek Squad branding but not get irritated by being held up. Stephens reckons that 10 times more drivers will see his cars than if he simply keeps up with the traffic flow.

The biggest challenge was finding the people who make the Geek Squad unique. Robert Stephens doesn't always have to pay top dollar: he says "that is the benefit you receive for having a remarkable culture." Instead, he looks for people who fit the DNA of the company. "If you get the right people they will work out the rest." He went on to say, "What unites us is that we all want an interesting life."

In 2002, the Geek Squad merged with Best Buy and opened Geek Squad precincts in all Best Buy US and Canadian stores. (The Special Agents who work in the Best Buy stores are called 'Counter Intelligence' of course!)

Today the company has 10,000 Geeks working out of 50 Geek Squad locations and in 700-plus Best Buy stores. Now that the firm has grown Stephens does invest in some marketing, and has a "Minister of Propaganda" to take care of that.

We asked him how he has managed to preserve the culture, despite having grown so rapidly. He told us that he sees his job is to "influence and inspire – I am not motivated by position or power, I just care about what we do and how we do it." One of the ways that the culture is reinforced is through a 24 hour hot-line that agents use to record and share their customer stories, called the "Squadcast." Another is through "hiring people for personality and their ability to innovate rather than technical ability – they can be taught that." The firm has steadied at a year-on-year growth rate of 40 per cent, but it will not hire people unless they are right.

WHAT ABOUT THE FUTURE?

Stephens predicts that we will see "widespread empathy." in other words, organizations really understanding the needs and wants of their customers and being able to meet these profitably. His vision for the Geek Squad is modest: "The complete and total world domination of the computer support business."

His biggest threat? "Our biggest competitor will always be ourselves because if we don't innovate then that will be our greatest threat."

This thirst for innovation led the Geek Squad to get into "cahoots with The Carphone Warehouse" another of our favorite brands. The Geek Squad will be helping The Carphone Warehouse to provide the same level of high-touch service to all customers in the UK.

Robert Stephens used all of the elements of See, Feel, Think, Do, but probably his greatest success factor was in recognizing the need in the first place. The Geek Squad is primarily B2C, high-tech, in your face, as American as it gets, and operates in a market with few credible competitors. Let's take a look at an organization that is much less visible but very successful. It operates in a highly performance and price-driven market and probably owes its current results to the gut feelings of one man.

CRC GROUP

CRC Group is a European-based organization that provides specialized after-market repair services for high-tech consumer goods. So CRC repairs products on behalf of brands like Nokia, Sun Microsystems, Siemens, and Hewlett-Packard. The market is fiercely competitive and driven by operational efficiency. Those companies that can provide the fastest turn-around times, highest first-time repair rates, and lowest costs win.

SEE

The story starts with Alan McLaughlin joining CRC as CEO in April 2002. He had done his "due diligence" before taking on the role, and knew that the company was in good shape. It had some very prestigious clients, a good reputation for quality, and a strong balance sheet. The company was turning over £100 million, and had a very strong relationship with Nokia, which accounted for about 70 percent of CRC turnover. Nokia was the market leader in mobile phones, and as it grew, so did CRC. As Alan did his rounds visiting investors and customers, it became clear that here was a business that was producing strong results on the back of excellent relationships. But something was troubling Alan.

FEEL

"I just felt that something was not right," he told us. Even though the relationship with Nokia was very strong and the numbers were all positive, the risk profile of the business left him feeling uneasy. As Alan started to form his strategy, he decided to make balancing the business his number one priority. He wanted to diversify so that less of the business was involved in high-tech consumer products, and more was in supporting older technology such as cash machines, point-of-sale terminals, and the like, because these products tend to produce much flatter workloads, unlike consumer goods, which tend to peak at certain times of the year. He also decided to reduce CRC's reliance on Nokia from 70 percent to 20 percent of turnover. The only way this balancing could be achieved quickly was by making acquisitions, and this was the strategy that he took to his board colleagues. They required some convincing, because the company was healthy, so why fix what wasn't broken?

Throughout 2002 the CRC team targeted a significant competitor called A Novo, but the complexity of the cross-border deal meant that ultimately it fell through. However, during the course of 2003 CRC targeted and acquired no less than three new companies, extending its reach into Europe as well as immediately acquiring some important customers in the high-tech consumer field and with slower-moving products. This was not a moment too soon.

THINK

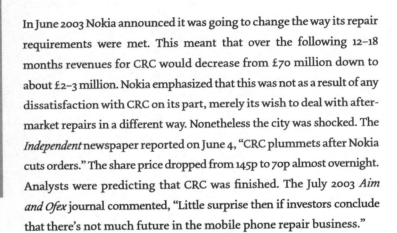

In June 2003 Nokia announced it was going to change the way its repair requirements were met. This meant that over the following 12–18 months revenues for CRC would decrease from £70 million down to about £2–3 million. Nokia emphasized that this was not as a result of any dissatisfaction with CRC on its part, merely its wish to deal with after-market repairs in a different way. Nonetheless the city was shocked. The *Independent* newspaper reported on June 4, "CRC plummets after Nokia cuts orders." The share price dropped from 145p to 70p almost overnight. Analysts were predicting that CRC was finished. The July 2003 *Aim and Ofex* journal commented, "Little surprise then if investors conclude that there's not much future in the mobile phone repair business."

Alan gathered his management team, and together they formulated a two-stage recovery strategy. The first phase was to take operating costs down to the level that could be supported by the reduced revenues. This resulted in closing a factory in Rugby and business in Northern Ireland, and a head count reduction of almost 20 percent. The second step was accelerating the alignment of the newly acquired businesses so that their contribution would compensate for the reduced revenues from Nokia as soon as possible.

DO

While the team was planning, Alan was on the road speaking with analysts, employees, and customers, to convince them that far from being finished, CRC had a very bright future. He spoke about his vision, the greater footprint in Europe, and better balanced portfolio. He asked for their support and the time to execute the strategy. The city responded. *Investors Chronicle* commented on August 29 of that year, "The market will need time to recover from the shock, but at least CRC has taken remedial action." By October of 2003 the share price had recovered to 110p.

The acquisitions that CRC made were strong companies with well-established customer bases. Even so Alan made a point of going out to meet with the customers and listen to their views. They told him that overall they were happy, but they were looking for improved turnaround times and greater responsiveness. As a result, teams were formed to re-engineer the existing processes to eliminate bottlenecks, increase flowthrough, and improve quality.

Alan installed a completely new senior management team for each business. He has a strong belief in the importance of the MD, HR director, and finance director working as a team (we use the term "triad power" to describe this), and feels that no matter how good the legacy management may be, you have to put in your own team that understands, and is committed to, the vision, strategy, and culture of the acquiring organization, so that they can quickly inculcate this throughout the new business.

The results were amazing. By the end of 2004 CRC turnover was back up to £69.3 million, down a mere 3 percent on the previous year despite having lost nearly 70 percent of its business as a result of reduced Nokia account. Net profit actually increased a massive 26 percent to £4.6 million. By February 2005 the share price had recovered to 247p and the *Investors Chronicle* was reporting, "With the Nokia disappointment firmly in the past and a solid business in place, prospects look bright for CRC. Buy."[49]

Despite this positive signal from the City, CRC remained in a highly competitive and volatile market. Alan McLaughlin knew that the company must continue to meet shareholder expectations if it was to thrive. Whilst progress had been made Alan remained uneasy because his gut still told him that the organization needed to be more efficient, more customer focused and prepared to shift the balance of its revenue from the very cost driven and cyclical IT repair business to more value added services. In the third quarter of 2005, a sharp decline in the IT repair business led to CRC issuing a profit warning. In October of that year Alan resigned. His worst fears had been realized.

We asked Alan McLaughlin what he had learnt from this situation.

Your gut instinct often operates as a leading indicator. Data is a lagging indicator. Trust your judgment.

What advice would he have for any other executive facing a similar situation?

Put on a life-jacket, batten down the hatches, and support your team whilst you ride out the storm, because it will get rough.

He went on to say, "But if you keep focused on your strategy you can achieve more than you ever believed was possible."

Once again, the CRC story illustrates each element of See, Feel, Think, Do, but in this case it was Feel that was the most important factor in determining the outcome.

CRC is a B2B business, and in a fast-moving industry. What about a highly mature market which is consumer driven, price sensitive, and in an area where culturally the management style is very traditional? How about a hotel and resort business in Turkey?

The Alarko-Hillside Leisure Group is one of the biggest and most reputable groups of companies in Turkey. Edip Ilkbahar is the founder and CEO of the Hillside Leisure Group, the leisure division of Alarko. The group portfolio includes management of the prestigious Hillside Beach Club at Fethiye, which is among the most expensive resorts in the Mediterranean.

When the Hillside Beach Club was created in 1994, the resort concept at that time was predominantly based on the holiday village model. The tried and tested formula consisted of inexpensive resorts, lots of activities, resort hosts who encouraged guests to join in the "fun," limited comfort, few facilities, and a mass approach to catering.

SEE

Mr Ilkbahar and his team decided to take a different approach. For some years they had run the management company of Pasha, one of the hottest of the mega nightclubs in Turkey. Mr Ilkbahar told us:

> Pasha gave us a chance to really get in touch with our target customer base and observe them in their own environment to see how they entertain, what they wear, what they find "cool" or "passé," how they react to circumstances. So we had a chance to engineer the whole concept of the resort according to these insights. This customer group is still the core of our guest base today.

But they were also very aware of the big picture. In any society there are major shifts in fashion and entertainment, and these trends shape expectations about what is "cool" and different. These were important objectives for the Hillside Beach Club.

From fashion to advertisements, from popular television shows to best-seller books, you can see major trends dominating. What we see as a change in our customer expectations are just a projection of one or more of these major trends. So starting from the first day, we decided to be aware of the world and customers in a broader sense, to understand the dynamics behind trends, and design our strategies and products accordingly.

This big-picture view coupled with in-depth engagement with the customers at Pasha created a rich source of data for the team. But at this point they were not ready to use formal research.

FEEL

The management team observed these potential customers and started coming to some important insights. "We felt that people didn't want to be in an atmosphere where organized activity is the sole driver. They want options for fun, but they want to feel in charge."

They realized that the customer, not the resort, must decide whether to join in the fun and activities, or to relax in a serene environment. The management team identified that customers actually wanted to experience some contradictory attributes:

Your product may be mass, but customer still want to feel as though they are getting personalized service. They want to be a part of a community, and they want to be remembered or known by name if they come again. They want to get professional service, but they want to be served by warm "owners of the house," not "professional staff."

So now they had the insight. Customers wanted a combination of access to fun, but choice about getting involved; a sense of community, but being treated as an individual; being served, yet not treated in a subservient way. But how could they turn this insight into a practical (and profitable!) business?

THINK

Mr Ilkbahar and his team thought laterally, and asked the question, "Why can't we create a resort that achieves all of these objectives?" In a perfect world the resort would be profitable because the rates are top of the market and yet it is always full – but how could they achieve both? To begin to answer these questions they engaged their people.

From the very beginning, the management team felt that they wanted to encourage a company culture of creativity and improvement. This was achieved by forming what they now call their "Dream Meeting." By bringing together a group of managers and employees who are continuously in touch with guests, who have an insight about customer requirements, and who know the operational limitations, they found that they could generate the most effective and practical ideas. This two-day "Dream Team" meeting has continued every year since to create new ideas for the Beach Club.

The Dream Team pondered this notion of how to be mass and boutique at the same time. The product had to be mass in terms of number of guests served, but create a real sense of being treated as an individual in the way that they were served. Mr Ilkbahar and his team took apart the guest "touch-line," and for each step, brainstormed how they could differentiate the experience. Ideas ranged from the minor – "We designed small but precious experiences for our guests, such as distribution of cold towels on the beach, and having our people wandering the beach cleaning sunglasses for guests" – to the major innovations like having a "movie night" with the screen literally floating on the sea, and astronomy classes with observations of the night sky.

One trend they noticed was greater environmental awareness, so the team started a scheme whereby a tree is planted for each guest, and the deed of the tree is presented to the guest as a memento at checkout. They started underwater yoga sessions, and the Holiday Club was the first spa resort in Turkey combining both Oriental and European architecture and service.

Finally, they created a concept they called "guest relations angels," staff whose only task was to be the interface between the operation and the guest. A guest at HBC is never forwarded to reception or any other relevant department for any special request; these requests are always handled by the appropriate guest relations angel.

DO

The major challenge for Mr Ilkbahar was to convince his people, both the top management of Hillside and some of the resort staff, that they could afford these innovations by achieving and sustaining a high price point, while their area, and Turkey in general, was becoming known as a cheap holiday destination.

For anything you want to achieve in business, you have to have your team believing in it first. In order to make them believe in it, you have to communicate your dream very clearly.

So to communicate the dream the company created a launch campaign and told the staff the vision: "Being number one in the Mediterranean." They told them about the credo: "Happy guest, happy company, and happy personnel." Most importantly the management team "walked the talk" and shared success with the staff. They even brought some of their junior employees from other locations to Istanbul in order for them to see for themselves the service provided in different top hotels and nightclubs, and to observe daily life so that they could form their own perceptions of consumer trends.

Of course they designed and delivered comprehensive motivation and training programs for all their people in order to create a common and shared corporate culture. These programs have become a continuing feature in HBC's success.

As we said earlier, the culture that the management wished to create was one of engagement, and so starting from the launch, they implemented a staff suggestion system which generates hundreds of staff suggestions each year. Any one of the employees can pick up the phone and leave a "better Hillside proposal" at an internal call center. They introduced a competition based on guest satisfaction surveys, so that functions and people began to compete to improve guest satisfaction.

So what were the results? Hillside Beach Club has become a success story in the region. It enjoys full occupancy for almost all of its season, in spite of room rates of up to US$500 per night for a regular room, which is at the top end of the market in Turkey, and rare for an 800-bed hotel. Nevertheless, guest surveys show that 95.5 percent of guests agree that they received "good value for money," with 97.5 percent saying they would "come again" and 99 percent saying they would "recommend" HBC to others. This is one of the highest advocacy levels we have come across. Clearly See, Feel, Think, Do have produced a great result for Hillside Beach Club.

We asked Mr Ilkbahar, how do you integrate traditional research with this more intuitive approach to business?

There are times you should use traditional research, like before opening a sports club in a new location; for testing a product, or exploring how deep a market is, but for creating new ideas experience marketing works best. The best way to convince people of this is to show that experience marketing works. Nothing is more effective than a business idea that achieves great success when it is implemented.

What about the future?

In today's world, we are all surrounded with information that is accessible to almost everybody all of the time. So creating a difference depends no longer on the amount of information you accumulate, but your ability to process information and reach an insight of what is really going on.

Thinking about how to differentiate was the key success factor for Hillside Beach Club, although all elements of See, Feel, Think, Do were addressed.

Robert Stephens said that the job of the CEO is to inspire and influence. Alan McLaughlin talked about supporting the team while "riding out the storm," and Edip Ilkbahar spoke of the importance of being different. All of these elements are illustrated in our next story.

We started this book by saying that See, Feel, Think, Do is about getting back to the fundamentals. It is not rocket science, and we certainly do not claim to have brought a new concept to the world's attention. Rather it is about stripping away the psycho-babble, consultant models, and endless analysis that is used in many organizations to fill a vacuum of leadership. This final story is about leadership.

It so happens that as we were finalizing for print in October 2005 there will be major celebrations for the greatest sea battle ever fought, and a commemoration of the death of Horatio Lord Nelson, Britain's greatest and most successful military hero. This book is first and foremost aimed at the business reader, but we believe the principals of See, Feel, Think, Do are as old as humankind, so we thought it would be interesting to apply them to a different kind of organization, place, and time. The organization is the British Royal Navy, and the place and time was Cape Trafalgar on October 20, 1805 the eve of the battle of Trafalgar. Believe it or not, See, Feel, Think and Do was very much on Admiral Lord Nelson's mind.

The Battle of Trafalgar was part of a much larger strategy to contain and ultimately defeat Napoleon Bonaparte, Emperor of France. 1803 saw the renewal of a long-running war between Great Britain and France and its ally Spain. It was clear that Napoleon's ambition was to occupy the British Isles and add it to his rapidly expanding empire. To that end he set about a rapid ship-building program, and massed 161,000 soldiers and 2,300 troop ships along the Mediterranean coast ready for the invasion.

SEE

In May 1803, Nelson was appointed commander-in-chief of Britain's Mediterranean fleet and given the task of blockading the French fleet, which lay at Toulon under the command of Admiral Villeneuve. However, Nelson saw the bigger picture. He realized that it was virtually impossible to guarantee being able remain on station in ships that were subject to the vagaries of the wind. He also knew that for as long as the French fleet was intact, so was Napoleon's dream of invading Britain. So his insight was not to contain the French, but to destroy them.

To do that he had to lure the French out. He said in a letter at the time to the Admiralty:

> *The Port of Toulon has never been blockaded by me: quite the reverse – every opportunity has been offered the Enemy to put to sea, for it is there that we hope to realize the hopes and expectations of our country.*

Nelson was very clear in his own mind what that hope was: "It is, as Mr. Pitt knows, annihilation that the Country wants."

Luring the French out was one thing; annihilating them quite another. Contrary to popular belief, most naval battles at that time were quite sedate affairs. In Nelson's time, navies would fight battles by forming their fleets into long lines, sailing past the enemy line, and firing. The smoke from the cannon made effective aiming almost impossible, and the damage to enemy vessels was frequently minimal, because of the inaccuracy of the guns and the strong reinforcement of the sides of the ships. In fact many more sailors were lost to shipwreck than enemy action, and fleet actions were generally inconclusive affairs.

Nelson, amongst others, had observed that the French used different tactics from the English. Whereas the English would aim at the hulls of the enemy in the hope of holing them and causing maximum casualties amongst the enemy seamen, the French would fire at the masts and rigging in order to disable the ships, and prevent their enemy from maneuvering so that they could then board them. The British had been at sea continuously for years. As a result the British seamen were highly trained, and led by seasoned officers, whereas the French had been hiding in port, and as a result, morale was low and their people were not as honed. Was there a way he could use all of these factors to create the "bloody and decisive" battle that he sought?

In March 1805 Nelson's blockade tactics worked. The French fleet led by Admiral Villeneuve broke out, and with favorable weather and too few British frigates available to scout, evaded the British fleet and headed for the West Indies. During the long chase that ensued, Nelson had plenty of time to ponder his question, and eventually an idea emerged.

FEEL

Nelson was driven by a deep-seated hatred of Napoleon, and he placed his own safety second to beating his enemy. His many wounds and scars were testament to the fact. He had fought and beaten

Villeneuve before, and knew that his enemy was formulaic and conservative as a commander. This time Nelson was determined to destroy him.

Nelson is known as much for his passion as his bravery. His love and infidelity with his mistress Emma Hamilton was scandalous at the time. He even wrote an impassioned letter on the eve of Trafalgar, leaving Emma Hamilton as a "legacy to the Nation" to try to gain her acceptance in society. And of course Nelson's last words to his trusted flag captain and life-long friend, "Kiss me Hardy," are the stuff of legend. This was a man who was in touch with his feelings.

During the long chase across the Atlantic and back in pursuit of the French, Nelson gathered together his captains, his "Band of Brothers" as he called them. Over a series of dinners he talked about his vision for the destruction of the French fleet and his insights of how it might be achieved. Together, using pepper pots and other tableware, they planned the battle. Nelson engaged his leaders in discussion of the different scenarios until they all fully understood his proposed new approach.

When Nelson rejoined the British fleet off Cadiz after a short leave, he spoke of the special bond between him and his "Band of Brothers."

The reception I met with on joining the Fleet caused the sweetest sensation of my life. The Officers, who came on board to welcome my return, forgot my rank as Commander-in-Chief in the enthusiasm with which they greeted me.

Nelson also cared deeply for the main body of his men, and knew many of them by name. His leadership style became known as the "Nelson touch." In an age when sailors had few rights, and were socially and hierarchically remote from their officers, Nelson earned not only the loyalty but also the love of his men. His concern for improving their food, working conditions, training, and well-being ensured that the front line were ready, able, and willing to follow his lead. His relationship was so strong that there were numerous reports of tough, battle-hardened sailors weeping upon hearing about his death.

THINK

Nelson realized that the destruction of the combined French and Spanish fleet would require a different way of fighting. He wanted to bring maximum destructive force to bear on the vulnerable bow and stern sections of the enemy, so he conceived an innovative strategy which was to sail at right angles to the enemy line, pierce it in three places, and surround the middle to bring about what he called "a pell-mell battle." This would disadvantage the more analytical and controlling style of his enemy, while favoring his own more fluid way of fighting.

Nelson's strategy required flawless execution and the total understanding and support of every sailor in his fleet, because it carried high risks. For the time it took for the British fleet to sail towards the combined French and Spanish line, they would be subjected to murderous cannon fire and unable to fire their own guns in return. Because of this Nelson knew that there was a very real personal risk, because he planned to lead one of the lines in his flagship, the *Victory*, and would be a prime target for the French sharp-shooters stationed in the rigging of the enemy ships. In fact, he had a premonition of his death, and shortly before the battle, bade farewell to one of his captains, saying "God bless you, Blackwood. I shall never speak to you again." Because of this he asked himself, how could he guarantee victory if he was killed? The answer was to make himself redundant.

During the course of his dinners with his captains Nelson spoke about his vision, outlined his strategy, and scribbled his plans on napkins. And when finally, every captain understood, he told them:

> *But, in case Signals can neither be seen or perfectly understood, no Captain can do very wrong if he places his Ship alongside that of an Enemy.*

He empowered independent action – unheard of in those days.

The British fleet finally tracked the combined French and Spanish fleet to Cadiz, and long months were spent trying to tempt the enemy out. All the while Nelson trained his men, exercising the great guns until their rate of fire was estimated to have been two, and in some cases three, times faster than their enemy.

Finally Napoleon, exasperated by the delay to the invasion, sent a message to Villeneuve advising him he was to be replaced as admiral of the fleet. The dishonor spurred Villeneuve to action, and finally, at 7.00 am on October 21, 1805, HMS *Sirius* on station off Cadiz signaled, "The enemy's ships are coming out of port."

Nelson formed his fleet of 27 ships of the line and got ready to take on the largest battle fleet ever assembled. Thirty-three ships formed the combined French-Spanish line, including the 130-gun *Santissima Trinidad*, the Spanish flagship and largest battleship in the world at that time.

Battle was joined, and as Nelson expected, the leading British ships came under withering fire. And then, at about 1.30 pm, a bullet from a French sniper's rifle entered above Nelson's left shoulder and pierced his backbone.

He lived long enough to learn of a great victory, though. The British fleet, although mauled, did not lose a single ship. The Combined fleet lost 20 ships destroyed or captured. France and Spain lost 4,408 men killed and 2,500 wounded, to the 449 killed and 1,200 wounded on the British side. In the words of Admiral Collingwood, Nelson's second in command, "The Combined Fleet is destroyed." Napoleon had lost his chance of invasion, and this was the beginning of the end for the Napoleonic Empire.

Nelson had been at sea since the age of 12, and even in his dying moments his expert eyes did not desert him. His last order to Captain Hardy was to anchor the moment the battle ended, because he predicted a great storm was coming. This final order saved a great many British lives. Shortly afterwards, at about 4.30 pm, Nelson uttered his last words, "Thank God I have done my duty," and died. While Nelson was a genius in all aspects of See, Feel, Think, and Do, his dying words sum up the key to success at Trafalgar: it was in the doing.

Rear Admiral Joseph F. Callo, in his book *Legacy of Leadership*,[50] imagined Lord Nelson being interviewed by a journalist and asked for his views on his success. These words seem a fitting way to end Nelson's story and this chapter.

> *Reporter: Sir, has advanced technology changed the kind of leaders needed in modern warfare?*
>
> *Nelson: ... A good battle plan can take you only so far. Once the event starts, decisions must be made in the midst of terrible violence. Those decisions can not be written into a plan,* **and they cannot be made by someone who is distant from the scene.** *It is on those decisions that the outcome of the battle ultimately rests.*

HOW TO SEE, FEEL, THINK, AND DO – THE TOOLKIT

Throughout this book we have used stories taken from history, movies, life, and of course business, to demonstrate what we mean by See, Feel, Think, Do marketing, because it is really understandable only through example. Similarly, it really only comes alive through experience. But how can you as a reader take the stories and the principles in this book and apply them practically in your business? Keeping in mind our normal caveats that this book is not a recipe book, and that these are guidelines for you to interpret in your own way, not hard and fast laws which must be followed religiously, we have nevertheless set out some simple tools and exercises that you can use to develop your skills at each stage of the See, Feel, Think, Do process.

SEE: "WALKING IN MOCCASINS"

EXPERT EYES

Interpret from your own accumulated experiences and intuition. Make sense of what you see by trusting your own judgment.

Suggested action

- Be a customer of your own brand for a day. Wake up one morning and go through the entire customer journey for your brand. Call your call center with a problem, visit a store incognito, make a reservation online. Use a notebook to make observations and comments about what you see and experience. At this stage you are walking in your customers' shoes, so don't try to rationalize, just experience it. Then do the same thing for your competitors. Compare the notes you have made. Be very specific about each stage of the customer journey you are making, and write your observations clearly. What are the hassles? Why? What were some of the differences in the experiences?

- Now go back over the journey, and using your expert eyes, examine each step in turn and analyze what went well, what did not, and what it would look like if it were better. What would you need to do operationally to improve the situation?

- Next time you are presented with a complex problem, allow your intuition to "flash" the solution. Now go through the usual process of analysis, problem solving and so on with your team, and when you are confident that you have the correct answer, reflect on how close or not your intuitive answer was. You may find that most of the time your intuition was right, and it is just a case of trusting it. The more you do this, the better you will get.

SOFT FOCUS

Don't treat observing your customers like a forensic, scientific investigation. Instead simply "experience" what they experience. See what is to be seen. Don't get in the way of yourself.

Suggested action

- Accompany your customers as they experience your brand. If your brand is a product, for example, watch them as they pick it up and look at it; ask them what they think about the product, how they use it. If your brand is a service, then sit on the plane or train or walk through the store with your customers. Observe what they get mad about, what delights them, what merely satisfies them. Watch their reactions to events and procedures. Ask them why they acted or reacted in the way they did. Strike up a conversation with them as fellow human beings, not as "consumers." You will often gain more real insights from one-on-one discussion with customers at the moment that they are actually buying or using your product than from a lot of focus groups held artificially and reported to you remotely.

- Identify a problem that you observed. Ask yourself the question, "How can we make this better for our customers?" If the answer isn't obvious or if the solution seems too difficult or expensive, write the problem and question down and put it away. Sleep on it, and from time to time contemplate the question from different aspects. Don't try to solve it, just let it come to mind at odd moments through the day. As you think about the problem, don't allow your mind to get too analytical or focus too clearly on it. Keep your focus soft and allow the answer to emerge. A good time to do this is when you are drifting off to sleep, in the bath or shaving, while listening to music – in fact any time that you cannot focus too intently on it. The answer will come when you least expect it – usually at about 3.00 in the morning!

- Buy a "stereogram" poster (or use the one on *www.seefeelthinkdo.com*) and practise using soft focus until you can switch between the design and hidden image at will. Use the same technique for observing a work situation that you know intimately. Try to see it in soft focus, and switch between seeing the obvious and the hidden or underlying issues. You may find that you will begin to notice things that you have never been aware of before.

BIG PICTURE

Link what you see to the "bigger picture."

Suggested action

- Look outside your industry and observe what is happening using the PESTLE dimensions as a framework. Think about the political, economic, social, technological, lifestyle, and environmental factors that you observe. Write a short description of what is happening under each heading, then ask, "What impact could this have on our business?"

- Look at the hard and soft data – sales, profits, growth, customer satisfaction, customer advocacy – that you use to run your business. Reduce these measures to the most important ones that directly impact your strategy, and create an experience scorecard to show how they are linked to the strategy, customer experience, and to each other. Regularly review this scorecard (weekly if needs be), and share it with your team. Don't use it as a stick to beat people with, but do ensure that the links between what is measured, the impact on the customer experience, and the results being achieved are made.

- Whenever you find yourself making a decision that is driven by short-term considerations, stop and ask, "What is the potential impact on our longer-term strategy or vision?" You may find that sometimes it is better to deal with the bigger underlying issue than try to fudge a short-term fix, even though it may cost you more in the short term.

Focus on what your customers are buying not what you are selling. For example, Häagen-Dazs may sell ice-cream in its retail stores but what the young couples who frequent the store are buying are "special moments." Lucio Rizzi, senior VP calls this "thinking outside of the scoop."

FEEL: YOU'RE A HUMAN BEING TOO

EMOTE

Don't be afraid to express or describe what you are feeling about a situation. It's what people do.

Suggested action

- Take a partner or a trusted colleague with you on an "experience trip" to visit customer sites, competitors, or best-in-class firms. Write down your feelings in your notebook, and share openly and honestly with your colleague or partner exactly how you feel. Don't rationalize your feelings, just express them and note them down.
- When presented with a situation at work, first tell people how you feel about it, then tell them what you think, or better still ask them.
- Sharing your feelings is particularly important when giving people feedback or appraising their performance. "I am very happy about the way that you dealt with that customer" is more motivating than "I think you dealt with that customer well." "I feel that you have let the team down" has more impact than "I think that you could have done better."

ENGAGE

Ask your customers to express their feelings.

Suggested action

- Rather than ask your customers to fill in a long survey form, interview your customers leaving a store and ask them how their experience was. Video their responses. Build this into a video vignette of your typical customer by segment. For each segment, show where they live, what brands they buy, what music they listen to, what they do for a living. Have them talk about their hopes and fears, frustrations and examples of great experiences. The intention here is to move from thinking about customers as markets to thinking about them as real people. These videos can be used for training and communication purposes in "Do."

- Provide an answerphone number that your customers can call if they wish to express their feelings about your service, but do not wish to speak to a person or require any action to be taken.
- Take your customers out for a drink or meal. When they are relaxed, ask them to open up to you about their feelings. Resist the temptation to rationalize or sell. Your job is to listen, restate, and empathize.

EMPATHIZE

Close the gap between what you feel and they feel. Understand how similar and different what they feel is from what you feel.

Suggested action

- Review the last conversation you had with a customer, and reflect on what you heard. Compare your feelings with those of your customer. If they differ, try to understand why the customer felt what he or she felt, or what exactly he or she meant by his/her descriptions. Listen intently. Your task is to understand, not justify.
- Think about a situation from your customers' perspective. Imagine you are a customer. Write down how you think they are feeling, what their view of you or your firm is. Try to capture their perspective succinctly. Now do the same looking at the situation from your perspective. Finally, imagine that you were an impartial observer asked to describe the situation. What might the observer say? Which is the most accurate perspective? The answer is usually somewhere near the observer's. This is a great way of empathizing and finding new ways of resolving dilemmas.

- When trying to resolve a problem with a customer, start by stating what you believe his or her perspective is, or feelings are, and ask for his or her response to check if you are right. If you are accurate, you are much more likely to reach a successful outcome than if you start out by stating your own perspective. If you are wrong, better to know that at the start of the conversation rather than find out later.

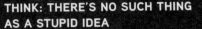 **THINK: THERE'S NO SUCH THING AS A STUPID IDEA**

CAUSE AND EFFECT

Interrogate like a child why things are the way they are. Be naïve in questioning what factors are affecting the moment that your customer experiences your brand.

Suggested action

- Ask the five "whys". First ask, "Why does this happen?" In response to that answer, ask, "Why does that happen?" Keep doing this until you get to the root cause of the problem. It should take five "whys" to reach the true root cause.
- Try saying "I don't know" occasionally in meetings, to create an atmosphere where new possibilities are discussed and leaders are not considered to be omnipotent. Ask questions if you know the answer but suspect that others may not. Junior people will often shy away from asking questions for fear of looking foolish.
- Think of outrageous opposites. Choose an issue or problem and then review the ideas that you came up with. Now brainstorm the opposite ideas. These may seem stupid or impossible, but they may stimulate the seed of an idea that could work.[51]

PERFECT WORLD

Think outside of the box. What is the perfect experience that we can bring customers?

Suggested action

- Taking each part of a customer's journey in turn and keeping your distinctive brand values in mind, brainstorm ideas to make your product or customer experience perfect. Don't be constrained by costs, historical precedent, or current realities.
- Go back over these ideas and select the ones that will differentiate your product or customer experience the most. Now think about the cost–benefit of introducing them, or finding lower-cost ways of achieving the same objective.
- Imagine you are a new competitor entering the market, and ask yourself how you could make the experience so much better for customers that they would desert the current suppliers. What would Richard Branson do if he came into your market?
- Use mind mapping to encourage creativity. If presenting your ideas, consider using mind mapping software like Mind Manager to help your audience see the big picture and visualize the perfect experience.

WHY AND WHY NOT?

Challenge how this would bring you and your customer real value, and challenge why it can't be done.

Suggested action

- Challenge received wisdom and assumptions. Don't accept things at face value. Ask, "Why do we do it that way?" "Why does it take us three days to approve a mortgage?"

- Use the same technique to brainstorm new ideas. In this case the question is, "Why can't we …?" as in, "Why can't we pay death benefit before death?"
- Get your team to work out two scenarios: what the uplift for the business would be if you delivered the improved customer experience, and what would be the impact on you if a competitor or a new entrant did it first.

DO: MAKE IT SO

NUTS AND BOLTS

What are the specific things we have to get right and put in place to make the perfect world a reality?

Suggested action

- Identify the new business model with associated processes, capabilities and skills required to operationalize your strategy.
- Create a cross-functional team at the highest level (heads of operations, marketing, HR, and so on), and get them to identify the precise tasks, targets, and timelines to implement the desired customer experience. Put a high-potential manager in charge of leading the initiative (not the person you can most easily spare).
- Walk the talk. Think of ways that you can personally demonstrate your own commitment to the initiative through your own behavior.

MAGIC DUST

How do we excite our customers about what we are offering and our people about delivering it?

Suggested action

- Create inspirational communication programs internally that will excite your people. Treat your employees as if they were customers, targeting their emotional needs and investing in the kind of high-quality, well-executed engaging communications that you would offer customers.
- Create "branded training" to bring alive the experience for your employees. Use experience marketing techniques to get them to really understand the "perfect world" you are trying to create for customers. Use the customer video vignettes to help communicate what your customers expect.
- Get employees to suggest ways of communicating the message to each other. Let them record a song, make a film. The way they communicate is not the way you communicate, and will be all the more powerful for it.

IS IT WORKING?

How do we know we have succeeded?

Suggested action

- Use a Customer Experience Management +™ survey (or similar) to assess the current experience that your customers have of you and their level of advocacy.
- Set relevant lead and lag targets focused on two sets of measures: first, customer advocacy (how delighted are our customers and how loyal are they?), and second, brand value (how much is our brand increasing in value as a result of our activities?).
- Find creative ways to reward results. The more creative and out of the norm the reward is, the more it will get the attention of your people.

Finally, practise using the See, Feel, Think, Do principles as you go about your business.

SEE

What am I experiencing? Buy a pocket dictaphone to describe in detail each moment of your visit to one of your offices or a depot, shop or customer experience journey. Record what you saw what you heard, what you smelt, what you thought; how you were greeted; how the product looked, what the advertising said, and so on. Use expert eyes and soft focus techniques. How does the experience relate to the big picture?

FEEL

What am I feeling? Describe your emotions at each stage of the customer journey. Do not rationalize them at first. How did I feel before I started the customer journey? How did this person or that thing make me feel? How long did that feeling last and why? What are other people feeling around me?

THINK

Why is this happening? Think about what is going on around you in the store, or what is happening on the phone. Why is it this way? What is the root cause of this issue? Think how you would like things to be different. What would be the perfect experience at every "moment of truth"? How can you turn this into a business opportunity?

DO

What do we do about it? Build a new business model and identify the capabilities required to operationalize it. Relate your vision and invite your team to work with you to plan the detailed steps to make it a reality. Get your team to work together to communicate the new direction internally and make it the reality.